# A MERCHANT SEAMAN'S SURVIVAL
An Autobiography

# AN ESCAPE STORY OF W.W.II
by Edward J. Sweeney

This book is dedicated to all Merchant Seamen who gave
their lives in the service of their country,
during World War 11. 1939 -1945.

1

# A MERCHANT SEAMAN'S SURVIVAL

A Merchant Seaman's Survival.
Published in England in 1999 by E . J. Sweeney,
44 Royal Esplanade Margate Kent. CT9 5EN.

ISBN No. 0 9536624 0 3
Printed in  England  by Lanes Printers, Broadstairs

Cover painting  by  kind  permission  of
Capt. Richard  Baker,  Auckland,  New Zealand.

# PREFACE

On September 1st 1939, Germany invaded Poland, and annexed the city of Danzig. This act of aggression occurred despite a previous agreement made with Adolph Hitler, the German Chancellor. Earlier, the British Prime Minister, Neville Chamberlain, arrived back in England, after an historic meeting with the Dictator. At the airport, the people waited eagerly for his arrival. Stepping from the plane, he gleefully waved high a signed agreement for all to see. He smiled as he predicted confidently, "There will be peace in our time". The large crowds cheered wildly at his announcement, but it was not to be. Hitler soon broke his word, resulting in the killing of 23,000,000 people during the whole of World War Two.

After the invasion, Great Britain strongly intimated that Adolph Hitler should withdraw his forces from Poland immediately, or suffer the consequences. By September 3rd, as these demands were not met, Neville Chamberlain broadcast his momentous announcement to the nation, "We are now at war with Germany". At the same time, 500,000 women and children were evacuated from the London area, to avoid possible bombing expeditions. Residents' gardens were dug, and small but adequate air raid shelters installed below ground level. They could cope efficiently with the blast from a nearby bomb explosion and its subsequent fallout. Rationing of some foods had begun, including bacon, butter and sugar. Soon Allied merchant ships would strive to keep up supplies. Otherwise, the population carried on normally.

The period became known as the phoney war, but it was not to last. In February 1940, the Government announced all merchant ships would be armed. Germany retaliated the next day, by confirming those vessels would be classed as warships and would be attacked.

During the first six months, over 400 merchant ships were lost through enemy action. The enemy's main objective was to cut off Britain's food supplies from overseas. The opinion of the British citizens suggested the war would be over by Christmas - an optimistic point of view.

It was not until May 1945, after a long bloody world war, that the Germans surrendered. Millions were killed before the Armistice was signed. The Japanese capitulated the following August, after the Americans dropped atom bombs on their cities.

The story I am about to tell relates to my wartime experiences as a 20 year old seaman.

I volunteered to rejoin the Merchant Service in 1940, after a 2½ year spell on "dry land." By the end of March 1940, there had been no call up of my age group for military service. The terrible actions and confrontations that took place at sea would soon change my life. It led to traumatic adventures and inhumane conditions, the like of which I could never have imagined.

It began with a losing sea battle with a German raider, and over eight months spent at sea in German ships. Imprisoned in a German camp in northern France, then escaping from a train travelling to Germany. There was a second escape from a concentration camp in southern France. After crossing the Pyrenees and being arrested, I was eventually released from the notorious labour camp at Miranda, Northern Spain. The events related are a true story of my adventures, still firmly entrenched in my memory. I can never forget the terribly degrading and inhuman treatment I received at the hands of other human beings.

E.J.S.

# ACKNOWLEDGEMENTS

I am forever grateful to Ms. Soubrier and family, for their help on my initial escape. My appreciation to Capt. Richard Baker, for permission to print his dramatic painting of the sinking of the SS "Turakina", to James Laird, and C. H. Milsom, Editor of Sea Breezes for their kind assistance. To P&0 Shipping for permission to quote from "Ordeal by Sea" and to publish the "Otranto". Also to George C. Shaw OBE (ex New Zealand Shipping Co. Supt.) for his contribution relating to the Company and the Pool. The Historical Branch of Internal Affairs, Wellington, for allowing assistance from "German Raiders of the Pacific."

Mdme Helene Jonqueres, Mediatheque, Perpignan La Catalane for her kind assistance. I'm also indebted to the Archives Dept. Perpignan. Des Pyranees-Orientale, France, and J. Guichoux, Mayor of St. Medard en Jalles. Also the Archives Departmentales, Bordeaux, Ms C. Voelckel, ex prisoner at Miranda. Thanks to J. W. Almond, ex "Rangitane", for his written permission to quote from his wartime experiences, and the personal photograph of the German raider "Komet". Also to John Quinn, Seddon Fenn, George Monk, T. Govier (Naval Network UK), and Edward Wilson for permission to publish German photographs from the Wilson collection, to Nucolorvue Productions Australia for the view of

Station Pier. Photographs of British warships and the "Pasteur", by courtesy of the Imperial War Museum. My appreciation also to Senor Louis Castro, Bergos, Spanish Professor of History. Acknowledgements also to R. M. Coppock, Naval Staff Duties, Ministry of Defence. There may be others I have failed to mention, if so, I would thank them all for the interest and encouragement shown while writing my story.

# Contents

# CHAPTER 1

## THE BLACK RAIDER

It was a cold miserable mid-winter's day at 6pm on the 18th August, when the "Turakina" sailed from the picturesque harbour of Sydney, bound for Wellington, New Zealand. I'd had a wonderful time in Australia, meeting again my former school companions, friends and distant relatives in Melbourne and Sydney. It was a poignant moment for me as I climbed the rickety wooden gangway to board the ship. Having to leave Australia again was not easy, but I consoled myself with the knowledge we were homeward bound.

Men who'd been ashore on leave had drunk a few beers in the nearby pub and were in a merry state. Not so the Captain, shouting angrily as he stood at the head of the gangway, awaiting the crew's arrival just a few minutes before sailing time. Those not required on watch, retired early to their bunks to sleep it off. As the ship sailed slowly from the harbour into the open sea, the weather worsened with very heavy seas running. In our quarters, being forward as far as one could possibly go, deck hands suffered the most discomfort, constantly tossed about

"TURAKINA"

From John Clarkson Collection

11

alarmingly during spells of stormy weather. However, there was no alternative, the conditions were part and parcel of the job, and accepted.

We had earlier called at Port Pirie in South Australia and loaded 4,000 tons of lead. At Melbourne Victoria, it was dried fruit and wheat, with lastly wool at Sydney, New South Wales. The "Turakina" was one of the few refrigerated vessels in existence. Ultimately, our cargo would be completed with the loading of frozen lamb from Wellington, New Zealand. The whole consignment was destined for Britain, where commodities such as meat and bacon and butter would be on ration.

It has been recorded that two thoroughbred horses were on board. One, a famous racehorse named Coronach, was a winner of the English Derby at Epsom, in 1926. It had won nearly £44,000 in prize money during its racing career. A considerable amount of money in those days. The other was a stallion called Golden Eagle, purchased for stud purposes. Both were being shipped to New Zealand.

It was perhaps an omen, on the night before the "Turakina" sailed from Sydney, a part of a movie was filmed by Argosy Films. Called the Power and the Glory, it concerned the achievements of the Merchant Navy during the early days of the second World War. It depicted the arrival on board of a German spy. It was also recorded at that time that the Radio Officer, S. Jones, had remarked that his job was too boring.

The crossing of the Tasman sea can be a daunting, frightening experience. Often, giant waves would reach heights of over forty feet. The tremendous force and battering received when ploughing through these heavy seas, would cause the ship to shudder from stem to stern as each wave struck. This was the scene as, with recurring cloudbursts of rain, the "Turakina" was spotted by the German raider, "Orion". Immediately she began to intercept our vessel.

The name "Orion" in Greek legend stands for a giant and hunter. It was perhaps appropriate that the "Orion" became known as the Black Raider. Built in 1930, she was originally a passenger ship of 7,021 tons, owned by the Hamburg American Line. First named "Kurmark", she was converted by the Germans to an armed cruiser. Officially called Shiff 36 during the conversion, on completion the name was changed to "Orion".

When the occasion demanded, she was able to take on the identity of ships of other nationalities, purely as a disguise. This was done by certain ingenious methods. An extra funnel could be erected, while the normal funnel could be reduced in height. Masts could be shortened or lengthened. Dummy deck houses could be quickly removed and positioned elsewhere. These were also used to hide the heavy guns from view. Being portable, the houses were shifted in seconds when action stations sounded. When masquerading as a British ship, a dummy gun would be erected in full view on the after deck.

D KURMARK

Even at sea, in all weathers, the German crew would carry out a complete repainting job. Hanging precariously over the side in their bosuns' chairs, the paint was slapped on with abandon and little finesse. New names were painted on the hull, combined with the corresponding national flag. The most commonly used disguise was Japanese, for at that time Japan was not at war with Great Britain and her Allies.

Whenever the "Orion" attacked, false names were quickly covered and the German Nazi flag flown from the mainmast. Disguised as the Dutch vessel "Beemsterdijk" of the Nederlands American Line, the "Orion" had embarked on April 6th 1940. It was the beginning of an amazing if often fortuitous campaign carried out by the Commander, Captain Kurt Weyher, and his stalwart crew. Their good luck saved them on many occasions, often being close to detection by searching Allied warships and aircraft.

Meanwhile, two further disguises were made. The first change was to the Russian ship "Cobet"; the second, to resemble the Greek vessel "Rokos". In the North Atlantic, on April 24th, their first victim was sighted. The "Haxby" 9,080 tons, was owned by the Ropner Shipping Company of Hartlepool, England. She had sailed from Glasgow, bound for an American port when she was intercepted. The "Haxby" was challenged and attempted to escape, so the "Orion" opened fire. As a result of the action, 17 British seamen lost their lives. A further 23 men were rescued by the Germans, and taken prisoner.

Once the survivors were taken on board, one torpedo was fired and the "Haxby" soon disappeared below the surface. The raider then gathered speed leaving the scene of the action, heading in a south-westerly direction.

The "Orion" was not a particularly fast ship, her maximum speed was probably around 15 knots. About three weeks later, in the south Atlantic, there was an arranged meeting with the German tanker "Winnetou". After taking on a full supply of oil, the vessels parted company. The "Orion" then sailed for the Pacific Ocean via Cape Horn. On reaching New Zealand waters, 228 mines were laid to the approaches of Auckland. While the mine laying was in progress, two warships, HMNZS "Achilles" and HMS "Hector" had sailed into Auckland. However, the Germans' good fortune held, and they remained undetected by the Allied naval vessels.

On the 19th June, leaving Auckland and bound for Vancouver, the "Niagara" 13,415 tons, hit two mines. A large passenger ship, owned by the Canadian Australasian Line, she eventually sank. Fortunately, there was no loss of life. Two other ships, the "Baltavia" 1,739 tons, and the "Port Bowen", were also sunk after hitting mines.

Meanwhile, the "Tropic Sea" 5,781 tons, had left Sydney bound for the UK. On the 19th June, the Norwegian ship was captured by the "Orion" and a prize crew put aboard. They sailed for Europe by way of Cape Horn.

On September 3rd, in the Bay of Biscay, she was challenged by the British submarine "Truant". The Germans scuttled the "Tropic Sea" and were apprehended by the "Truant", then put ashore in Spain. Being released in a neutral country, all the prisoners, British, Norwegians and Germans, eventually reached their respective homelands.

For many weeks, the "Orion" scoured the sea routes for further victims without success. However, on the 16th August, a small French ship the "Notou", 2,489 tons, was intercepted. She was headed for Noumea in French Caledonia, carrying 3,900 tons of coal loaded at Newcastle, Australia. Thirty eight prisoners were taken and their ship sunk by explosives and gunfire.

The "Orion" then sailed for the Tasman Sea between New Zealand and Australia. Four days later, in very bad weather, there came the fateful sighting of my ship, the "Turakina". It resulted in a battle fought against overwhelming odds, and for me, the beginning of an incredible adventure that would last another twelve months.

# THE NEW ZEALAND SHIPPING CO.
# &
# THE MERCHANT NAVY POOL

The Company was founded at Christchurch New Zealand in 1873, with the sole purpose of competing with the Shaw Savill and Albion Companies which were also operating on the United Kingdom run. The Federal Steam Navigation Company (FSN) was formed by shipping magnate Allen Hughes in 1895 and it became a subsidiary of the New Zealand Shipping Company in 1912. Both companies were subsequently taken over by P&0 cargo division in 1916, the first of a rapid series of mid-war acquisitions organised by Lord Inchcape.

Although FSN kept its identity for accounting purposes and were listed as owners in Federal colours, they were totally associated with the NZSC for Management and Superintendence. After World War Two everything was fully integrated and three tankers, the "Lincoln", "Derby" and "Kent", were built around 1958, operating in the Federal colours. The New Zealand Shipping Co., changed their traditional yellow funnel in passenger ships, to what was thought to be the more dynamic colours of Federal. The story goes that the latter originally had a St. George Cross flag, but the Royal Naval Authorities objected. Somebody hurriedly sewed a square of blue in the centre, and the distinctive colours were born. Correspondence at senior management level still reflected the separate corporate status and dock office letters were still headed by the names of the two Companies until September 1971. On that date, they became a part of P&0 Deep Sea Cargo Division.

At the outbreak of the second World War, the New Zealand Shipping Company and the Federal Steam Navigation Company had a combined fleet of 31 ships. Seven were passenger vessels, including the SS "Ruahine", which was laid up at Falmouth, Cornwall. Although most were registered in Plymouth Devon, their home port was the Royal Albert Dock, London E16.

The Superintendents' Department was housed in a corrugated iron building opposite No. 25 shed. The Import Department office stood opposite No. 33 shed, which, together with No. 29 shed, were the principal discharging berths. At the time, Captain H. Dawson was Marine Superintendent in overall charge of the dock office, where a wide range of ship husbanding and management functions were carried out. It included the loading and discharging of cargoes and the embarkation and disembarkation of passengers. In addition to Captain Dawson's Department, others were headed by the Supt. Engineer, Naval Architect, Radio Supt., Victualling Supt. and an Export and Import Supt.

Although ship repairs were carried out by Contractors, the Company had a policy of employing its own staff and labour for a whole range of activities. This required a large number of workshops, stores and cribs to house the staff. It included the shore carpenter, wiremen and the rope makers who made up and supplied the ships with their special requirements, including rope ladders and lifeboat gear. A sail maker was employed putting together a variety of canvas goods particular to a ship's special needs. The shore carpenter provided the screens and partitioning needed for making accommodation between decks for emigrants.

Another feature was the linen room, where seamstresses repaired and sorted linen for laundering and organised the returning of the hundreds of sheets, towels, pantry cloths etc. for the next outward voyage. The Company also engaged their own dockers and stevedores, so it was necessary to stock and maintain the enormous amount of cargo equipment required for handling the different types of cargo. The electric bogey trucks in use needed an extremely large battery charging facility.

With this hive of activity, it was necessary to employ a casual shore gang of about one hundred hands under the command of a hard-bitten shore Bosun. These were the Marine Superintendents' right hand men, clearing up the mess left by others. The work included mooring and un-mooring ships right round the clock, seeing to stores, cleaning holds, lashing cargoes and laying and lifting dunnage. There was also an engine room gang under the supervision of a foreman. Their tasks included handling a variety of jobs in the tanks and the engine room and tending to equipment and boilers in port, while the crew were on leave.

Dockers and stevedores were taken on at a morning and afternoon "call", just inside Connaught gate near No. 33 shed. This area, like most of the dock roads, was cobbled, and men not required, were said to be "left on the cobbles."

Cockney rhyming slang and banter was common between the shipworkers and Company staff, and anyone not up to scratch was threatened with "the Cobblers." The amount of cargo handled by the various gangs was estimated by tally clerks. Piece work rates were worked out by cashiers for each work session and paid when the brass tallies were handed in. Any delay in payment would be met by a loud chorus of protest.

The four companies that dominated the New Zealand and Australian trades were the Blue Star, NZSC, Port Line, Shaw Savill and Albion, and the FSNC. They came through the catastrophic slump of the 1930's in much better shape than many others. Ships laid up in dock were a common sight and wages were reduced by 10% in 1932 because of the recession. This cut was restored in 1937 and by 1939, an AB's pay was £9.12.6 (£9.62½p) per month, all found on board.

The Companies were among the first to recognise the National Maritime Board which was created in 1920. At the time, it was described as the first real experiment in industrial self-government for the industry, purely on a voluntary basis. In effect, it meant that when it became a question of employment of ratings, it would be a closed shop, with membership of a Seamen's union mandatory. Almost all seamen were domiciled in the U.K.

The engagement of ratings was formalised through the Joint Supply System, operated by the Shipping Federation, (A sort of Shipowners' Trade Association) and the National Union of Seamen. The very nature of shipping meant casual employment for seafarers was normal, generally with no pay between voyages. New Zealand Shipping had a policy of providing as much continuity as possible. Fortunately, the UK's dependence on a cheap food policy meant a steady trade with primary producers such as Australia and New Zealand. Both countries at the time relied heavily and exclusively on UK manufactured goods. All these items attracted relatively high freight rates.

In 1929, there came the introduction of the three "Rangi" class ships. With nearly 250 crew required for the 600 passengers aboard, a small team operated in the Marine Department. They were responsible for checking wage calculations and the paying of cash when the ship "paid off". On signing on again, allotment notes were provided. These were a feature of a seaman's employment and were in great demand. Their objective was to provide money for the couple of weeks they had been without pay. This advance note was only payable three days after the ship sailed, provided that the recipient had rejoined his ship.

To realise instant cash, it was necessary to change it with an Advance Note Discounter, who would charge two shillings, (10 pence) in the pound. This was to cover the risk of a man jumping ship prior to sailing. He was referred to as "The Cracker", as he cracked the Advance note. There were other uncomplimentary remarks regarding his rate charge.

Many of the deck hands were from the Western Scottish Isles, mostly from Stornoway, and were generally known as "Stornowegians". Between voyages, particularly in summer, more frequent lay ups occurred. This was due to the lessening of shipments following the peak cropping period of the Australian and New Zealand fruit harvest. The men would return home to go crofting or fishing and would often come back with a couple of younger relatives hoping to be engaged and begin a life at sea. There was little alternative work available in the Isles.

They would find accommodation at a local Seamen's Mission along with young Ordinary Seamen awaiting reappointment. Deck boys just out of Sea School were also provided shelter and employed in the "Yard" under the supervision of the yard Bosun. I would usually be detailed to act as a stand-by messenger, taking written and verbal communications to ships around the docks. This was before the widespread use of telephones. On the message being delivered, it was always compulsory to say, "Captain or Mr . . . . . presents his compliments, and would you please. . . . . . !"

When the Company needed to engage deck ratings, they contacted the Shipping Federation office at Connaught Rd. Through the grapevine and the little black book, the officials were aware of whom not to send. The Marine Department hired the seaman, who would then be examined by the Shipping Federation Doctor. If passed, he would be cleared by the Union, whose main task was to clear any outstanding Union fees, usually by means of their Advance Note. The Company would agree to deduct weekly subscriptions for the Union, providing the individual signed the necessary paperwork. The list was delivered to the office by an official on a bicycle just prior to the ship's sailing. Some of these officials actually became leading lights of the Union movement in the post-war years.

Once cleared by the Union, the rating was issued with a large white PC5 form, similar in size to the old £5 note of that era. This form was actually the passport to signing Articles of Agreement at the nearby Mercantile Marine Office, also in Connaught Rd. It was an imposing building compared to the old corrugated iron offices of the Shipping Federation and Seamen's Union, whose postal address was in fact, "The Hut".

The Mercantile Marine Office was the focal point for the signing on and paying off of seafarers under the comprehensive legislation of the Merchant Shipping Act.

All documentation in this connection was sent to the offices of the Registrar-General of Shipping and Seamen, based at Tower Hill, London. In 1940, during the war, the offices were evacuated to Cardiff, where they remain to this day.

Documentation would be received from M. N. Offices or Custom Houses from every port in the United Kingdom. If a seaman joined or left a ship abroad, details were sent to Cardiff, enabling records to be kept up to date. It was essential in times of war to know precisely who were actually on board in case of a sinking. The NZSC also kept their own records, updated by cables from Shipping Agents, when changes abroad took place.

The Mercantile Marine Office would post a list of ships that were signing-on and had vacancies. Crews would be mustered for selection, but the prospect of an untrained youngster shipping out without going through the Joint Supply System had long gone. Every member of the crew was required to sign on in the presence of a Superintendent of the M.M.O. He was usually referred to as the Shipping Master. Two sets of the Articles of Agreement had to be signed. A black set was kept by the Master until the final payoff, while the red set was forwarded to the Registrar-General.

The Merchant Shipping Act specified that certain officers and ratings should hold relevant certificates issued by the Board of Trade. Until these requirements were met, the Superintendent would not issue a further certificate to the

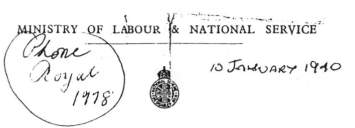

# MINISTRY OF LABOUR & NATIONAL SERVICE

*Phone*
*Royal*
*1778*

*10 JANUARY 1940*

**BARKING ROAD EAST HAM E.**

DEAR SIR,

In view of the urgent need for young men in the Forces, the Government has decided, as already announced in the Press, that deferments granted for the younger men in certain occupations must be brought to an end. The enclosed summons to medical examination is issued as a preparatory step to calling you up, if medically fit, for military service. You will not, however, be called up until after your employer has received a letter from the District Man Power Board relating to you, and other workers in his employment, covered by this decision. You will not, therefore, be called up immediately, and in any event you will receive at least six days notice of call up.

**Please show this letter to your employer.**

Yours faithfully,

Note.—Employers should not at this stage enter into correspondence with this Department about any individual to whom this letter relates. All employers concerned will be communicated with before any action is taken to call up any man concerned.

M21715  50M  11/42  C.N.&Co.Ltd.  749 (897)

ship's Captain for sailing until cleared by the Custom House. It also specified a certain number of certificated lifeboatmen for each passenger ship. If a Royal Naval Reserve Master wished to fly the Blue Ensign flag, some R.N.R personnel also had to be engaged throughout the voyage.

Every seaman was issued with his own discharge book, often referred to as a CD (Continuous Discharge rather than Single Voyage Paper Discharge). Masters would report to the Marine office on the conduct and ability of their crews and the Shipping Masters had special stamps to fit in the appropriate spaces in their reports. Reports were categorised: "Good", "Very Good", "Decline to report", "Voyage not completed", or "Endorsement not required". Those with anything other than "Very good" were politely informed they would not be required for the next voyage. Subsequently, it would become very difficult for them to find new employment.

At the outbreak of war, Royal Navy Reserve Officers were called up for service. Those on leave were mobilised immediately; the others, when their ships returned to the UK. However, it was imperative to keep the ships manned after the loss of such key personnel. The Shipping Federation repeatedly warned the Board of Trade, the Admiralty and Minister of Co-ordination of Defence of the danger of insufficient manpower. An official announcement was made, "It is desired to emphasise, that all those who are, or have recently been serving in British merchant ships cannot do better than hold themselves available to continue in this essential national service".

From the outset, the Merchant Navy was listed in the schedule of reserved occupations. Seamen were given their own official badge to show the importance of their service and the risks being taken. Wearing the badge also indicated that, although in civilian clothes, the men were still serving their country. There was a mad scramble for manpower by all the essential industries, while ships were held up for lack of crews. It became obvious that something drastic had to be done to ensure that seafarers were reserved exclusively for sea service.

On the 30th April 1941, the Ministry of Labour signed the Essential Work (Merchant Navy) Order, and so introduced the Merchant Navy Reserve Pool. Seamen were prohibited from leaving the shipping industry but, to their advantage, between engagements there would be guaranteed pay and adequate leave for the first time.

The "Turakina" was one of the first ships to berth in the Royal Albert Dock after war was declared. Captain Laird thought he would outwit the enemy by painting out the first T and last A to become the "Urakin". Also the word New was added to the registration port of Plymouth, making it New Plymouth, which it was hoped the enemy would presume to be in a neutral country.

In May 1940, after the fall of France, it was unsafe for ships to be routed via the English Channel. They were forced to sail round the north of Scotland, and down the east coast. They then faced the risk of U Boats, E Boats, bombers and mines.

The "Remuera", a NZSC passenger ship, built in 1911, and a survivor of World War One, was sunk by bombers off the east coast of Scotland. This almost signalled the end of this route and no more of the Company's ships were to visit the Royal Albert Dock for many years.

The final blow to the docks came on the afternoon of Saturday, 7th September 1940, when German bombers devastated the area during one of the heaviest daylight raids of the war. They continued to pound the East End of London, its docks and the homes of the many people who lived and worked there. These massive raids occurred regularly every night for three months. The dock offices escaped major damage, but the stores were hit, much to the Storekeeper's distress. Scattered everywhere were his hoarding of treasured pieces of equipment from ships long gone, together with baggage and gear left over the years by Officers for safe keeping.

The damage to essential services was severe, while for some time there was no gas, electricity or telephone available. During the continuous bombing, two ships were tied up. The "Otaio" was in Victoria dock when it was struck by a bomb that penetrated three decks yet failed to explode. The "Surrey" was discharging at Royal Albert Dock and endured the raids until she sailed on the

27th September. At one stage her rudder suffered problems due to the near misses.

The docks were severely damaged in places and workers' homes were demolished. For many, their jobs had also gone up in smoke. Some dispersed, but in the case of the Company's import and export staff, they were relocated in the west coast ports, where cargo operations were carried out for the remainder of the war. Although much of the Superintendence would be carried out from the Liverpool office, it was decided the dock office in London should continue to function. Recruitment was done through the Shipping Federation at Connaught Rd, while Articles of Agreement were often signed in the Mercantile Marine office.

They were soon involved in dealing with crews whose ships had sunk. In peacetime, a shipwrecked seaman was entitled to draw wages from the shipowner until he joined another vessel. The maximum period for payment was two months. It was soon realised that this would not be a satisfactory arrangement, particularly where prisoners-of war were concerned. A detailed wartime agreement was negotiated with the Government in 1939. Shipping Federation offices became responsible for handling the payments of Seafarers' Unemployment Indemnity, which was due from the day that the ship sank. They also ensured that when shipwrecked persons reached the UK they were well looked after and immediately placed in funds.

Many of the liner Companies took on added responsibilities through their own organisation, but there is no doubt uncertainties and confusion brought about many losses in tramp ships, causing distress to both the men and their families. A spate of losses in the larger companies meant that Petty Officers, Leading Hands and specialists in the Catering Dept. found it difficult to obtain similar pay and conditions. Another problem related to compensation for loss of effects. There was a sliding scale, depending on rank or rating, but the sums involved were far too low. It by no means covered those men serving in ships for years, literally building their homes around them.

Much has been made of statements in certain documents about the Merchant Navy, which indicate that pay ceased on the day of the ship's sinking, with the seaman left destitute after facing so many dangers. The Company had to account to the crew for wages and deductions from the time of signing on until the day the tragedy occurred. These payments would normally be made in the presence of the Superintendent of a Mercantile Marine office. He had to be satisfied that the deductions were correct under the relevant Merchant Shipping Act. Also, he would ensure that true amounts were paid for those who had died and for those presumed lost at sea.

In some instances, the Articles of Agreement had gone down with the ship together with the wages book and lists of cash advances etc. In such cases, the red set was obtained from the Registrar-General of Shipping and

Seamen. Calculations and deductions would then be made in accordance with the cash vouchers and receipts sent home prior to the loss of the ship. Many cases were relatively simple to sort out quickly. Others, like the "Turakina" and the "Rangitane", where the crews became prisoners-of war, were more difficult to resolve. Only those who were captured and their families know the full drama and uncertainty of their circumstances.

# CHAPTER 2


# THE EARLY DAYS


During World War I, my father, Timothy Patrick Sweeney, served as a seaman in the British Merchant Service. Jumping ship in Melbourne Australia, he volunteered to join the Australian army. On 23rd June 1916, he enlisted as a gunner in the Field Artillery, 15th Battery, 6/4 Brigade. Sent overseas to France to help combat the Germans, he fought for two years in fields and trenches in the mire and slush of the battlefields of the Somme, Flanders and Ypres.

With his khaki uniform he wore a bandoleer (a shoulder strap containing ammunition) and a broad brimmed hat turned up on one side. On the battlefield he would wear brown leather leggings and brass spurs. The latter were used to urge on the horses while attempting to drag the heavy gun carriages through the thick, sticky mud that prevailed. This happened frequently, as the opposing armies would retreat and advance at regular intervals, causing thousands of casualties. In 1932 at the age of 40, after a long illness, he died as a direct result of injuries received during the war years.

I was born in Port Melbourne in the garden State of Victoria, Australia on the American Day of Independence, July 4th 1920. We lived near the seafront in a small colonial type house with decorative wrought iron work and a veranda built on the front. Like most of these properties, the roof consisted of heavy corrugated metal sheets. During the very humid summer weather, often with temperatures of 43 degrees, the inside became unbearable, particularly when hot dusty north winds prevailed. There was no air conditioning at that time. In the winter months, the heavy rainstorms would relentlessly beat down on the metal roof, the resounding clattering making it impossible to sleep.

If milk were needed, I would walk to the nearby dairy in Graham Street, carrying my mother's china jug. From a large churn Mr. Williams would ladle one quart, which I would carefully carry back home. As my Father was unable to work due to ill health, money was in very short supply. There was no help in those days from the State, so it was necessary for my mother to do cleaning work. It was some years before a War Widow's pension was finally awarded.

To help out, after school I would sometimes visit the local abattoir with a few boys of my age. We watched and waited while animals were slaughtered and hung. As meat was very cheap and in abundance, offal was rarely saved. The concrete floors were hosed down and the staff would throw us the livers, kidneys, tripe etc., which I would then collect and wrap in newspaper. Although the offal provided a welcome and nourishing addition to our diet, I hated the visits to the slaughterhouse.

Opposite our house in Princes Street, stood Borer's the bakers. Oblong shaped loaves (known as tinned), would be loaded on to a bread cart, pulled by a solitary horse. The unwrapped loaves, stacked on large wooden trays, were then delivered to the grocery shops in the area. Needless to say, we purchased the freshly baked hot loaves directly from the bakehouse. On occasions, the baker, knowing our circumstances, would give me a loaf free of charge. A few doors away was Perazzo's fish and chip shop. There we could buy potato cakes. They consisted of giant sized slices of potato, fried in crispy batter. As they always tasted so delicious, I often wondered why they were never available in the UK. Maybe they are, but in all my time here I have never seen them. Perhaps they're much too fattening - if my memory serves me well, most members of the Perrazzo family weighed about 18 stone.

Instead of a refrigerator, we possessed an icebox. It was a tall chest, with a separate lined space in the top. The iceman, with a sack over his shoulder, would deliver a large solid block of ice. With the aid of an ice pick, he would gently lower the heavy block into the top compartment. As the ice slowly melted, it would drip into an enamel container underneath. It was quite successful, with the ice lasting about three weeks. It was not expensive to operate, as no electricity was required. It was my job to empty the bowl and ensure it didn't overflow.

Melbourne was only a short distance away, reached by either cable tram or electric train. Sometimes my father would take me to the State theatre in the city to see a silent film with stars such as Harold Lloyd, Buster Keaton or Charlie Chaplin. The alternative would be a cowboy and Indian epic. We possessed a crystal wireless set my Father had constructed. Wearing earphones, he would spend many hours listening whilst patiently using the cat's whisker to tune into broadcasts from the radio stations 3L0, 3AR or 3DB.

In the 1920s, Port Melbourne was a busy thriving locality. It was the heyday of the majestic passenger liner and huge cargo vessels. A constant stream of ships from all corners of the globe would berth at Station pier. Australia had in force the White Australian Policy, barring coloured people entering the Continent. "White" people wishing to emigrate to Australia could easily obtain an assisted passage. Successful applicants from Britain would pay just £10 for the voyage.

The port was situated close to the mouth of the Yarra river, the gateway to the steadily growing city of Melbourne, capital of the southern State of Victoria. Numerous vessels would sail up the river to the Victoria

STATION PIER — PORT MELBOURNE

docks, in close proximity to the city. Living in this environment, with a five minute walk to the beach, was the beginning of a long association with ships and a love of the oceans. So much so, that practically all of my life I have lived in sight of the sea.

As a young fresh faced schoolboy, I was fascinated watching the departure and arrival of the large passenger and cargo ships.

On occasions, a small fishing boat would unload its catch. It was fascinating to watch the fishermen haul onto the pier three or four fearsome looking monsters such as grey nurse or tiger sharks. Some specimens would be four to five metres in length. It was not uncommon for us to dive off the pier to swim as we never dreamed we would be attacked by sharks. Now, I think how foolhardy we were.

I would sit on the pier, dangling my feet over the edge, watching intently for hours while the huge cranes and burly stevedores performed the duties of loading and unloading of the various cargoes. I would notice the happy faces of the passengers going ashore and dreamed that one day, I too would become a passenger on a huge ocean going liner. The six week journey to England, 12,000 miles away, was always in my thoughts. Some years later, the dream was realised, but the circumstances would be entirely different to those I had imagined.

I particularly remember two impressive American white passenger liners that regularly berthed at the port. They were the "Mariposa" and the "Monterey". Other regular ships to call were those of the P&O line. These included the "Orama", "Orcades", "Oronsay", "Otranto", "Ormonde" and the "Orion" which were very large passenger ships of approximately 20,000 tons. Another vessel I remember well was the "Ceramic", of the Blue Funnel Line. At the time, she was said to be the longest passenger/cargo vessel to visit Australia. Unfortunately, she was sunk during the war in December 1942, with most of the crew killed.

Other vessels on the Australia and New Zealand route belonged to the Shaw Savill and New Zealand Shipping Companies. I can also vividly recall the "Bay" boats; four passenger vessels with a distinctive bright green painted hull and a single yellow funnel. Owned by the Aberdeen and Commonwealth Line, the fleet included the "Jervis Bay", "Moreton Bay", "Largs Bay" and "Esperence Bay". A few years later, I was destined to join the crew of the "Largs Bay", making my first trip to sea. During the war, the "Jervis Bay" was converted to an armed cruiser and was on convoy duty when she was attacked and sunk by a German battleship.

At the age of eleven, I graduated from Nott St. State school in Port Melbourne and was attending the South Melbourne Technical College. One master was known by the name of Major Drummy. On being installed in his class, he informed us that he expected an excellent standard of work and that we should always remember to keep cool, calm, composed and collected. Any problems

ORIENT LINE. S.S. OTRANTO. 20,000 TONS.

and we would be shaking hands with Oscar. "By the way", he said, "Have you met him?" From behind his back, he produced a thick leather strap and said, in a quiet sarcastic voice, "Let me introduce you to Oscar." Anyone who was brave enough to talk in class was liable to have a 15cm wooden blackboard duster whistle past their ear.

Our Headmaster was known by the schoolboys as "Shot Elliott". We assumed it meant he was a good shot with the strap. I confirmed that we were right when I was punished for repeatedly throwing stones on somebody's corrugated iron roof. Upon being identified by the occupant during assembly in the quadrangle, I was summoned to the Headmaster's office, where I admitted my guilt. I had my right sleeve rolled up and received "six of the best". His aim was good and he certainly didn't miss. A painful lesson was learned however, and I never repeated the incidents that occurred at No. 6 Dundas Place, South Melbourne. Nor have I ever forgotten my punishment, the first and last time that I received the strap.

After the death of my father, having few close relatives in Australia, my mother thought it wise to return to England. At the age of 14, I was about to leave the land of my birth and begin a new life in a strange country. I was not looking forward to the prospect, particularly the thought of the colder winters. Passages were booked on the majestic Orient liner "Otranto", sailing from Port Melbourne on 29th May 1934. Although overawed at the size of the ship, crossing the gangway and going on board was a sad time for me. I shed a few tears as two busy tugs towed us free of the pier out into the choppy waters of Port Phillip Bay.

I remembered the happy day-trips spent on the paddle steamers "Hygea" and "Weroona", landing at the seaside resorts of Queenscliff or Sorrento further round the Bay. From Station pier there was a good Australian send off, with colourful streamers in abundance. I waved frantically to my school friends until they were out of sight. I thought I might never see them again. My sadness was soon forgotten as I wandered about the huge ship, getting my bearings. The cruise proved to be an exciting experience, visiting countries I had only dreamed about. At the age of 14, my earlier childhood wish had been fulfilled.

# ITCHY FEET

I had lived in England for almost two years and had begun to miss my homeland. I yearned to revisit sunny Australia to meet all my ex school friends. My solution was to enlist in the Merchant Service. I had just turned sixteen when I signed on with the "Largs Bay" as a deck boy (trainee seaman).

An uncle of mine, Mick Aherne, was the ship's bosun. Using his influence, he helped in my efforts to enlist. However, although related, he never spoke to me throughout the whole voyage. I expect it was to show that there was no favouritism. I had enjoyed the life at sea and looked forward to a second trip on the "Largs Bay". At the end of each long voyage it was the normal procedure for all crews to be discharged.

By this arrangement the shipping companies were not obliged to pay their employees while the ship was laid up, even if only for a few weeks. On rejoining, it meant signing a new contract. After docking at the Royal Albert/King George V docks in London, I inquired if I could rejoin the "Largs Bay" on her next voyage. The answer was an emphatic refusal. On asking the reason,

44

AKAROA 1937

45

E. J. SWEENEY 1937

the reply was, "You spent too much time playing table tennis with the passengers!" Nevertheless, I'd had a wonderful time seeing all my friends in Melbourne and found I had an overwhelming urge to see more of the world. Feeling rather upset and scared at my uncle's possible reaction to the news of my dismissal, I decided to use my initiative and endeavoured to sign on with another Company.

In Connaught Road, was the bare dingy premises of the Shipping Federation. Feeling rather apprehensive, I presented myself to an official, explaining my reasons for wanting another ship. I needn't have worried as there was an offer of employment with the Union Castle line, sailing to Buenos Aires, South America. However, I declined the proposal as I rather preferred the Australia run.

There were no vacancies on any Australia bound ships, but there was an opportunity of a trip to New Zealand. I accepted that suggestion, thinking of the wonderful scenery when sailing through the Panama canal. I decided to postpone my original plan, as a trip to Melbourne could be made another time. I agreed to sign on as a deck boy to continue my training. My second ship was the passenger/cargo vessel, "Akaroa", owned by the Shaw Savill Company. At the time, she was the flagship, operating a regular service between New Zealand and the United Kingdom.

ISSUED BY THE BOARD OF TRADE, In pursuance of 57 & 58 Vict. ch. 60.

# ACCOUNT OF WAGES. F.

| Name of Ship | Official Number | Description of Voyage or Employment |
|---|---|---|
| "AKAROA" | 133648 | N.Z. |

| Name of Seaman | Refr. No. in Agreement | Date and Port of Engagement | Date of Discharge | Rate of Wages |
|---|---|---|---|---|
| E.J.Sweeney | 38 | 6. 8. 1937. London. | Nov. 1937 | £3.0.0. |

14 NOV 1937

| Earnings | Amount | | | Deductions | Amount | | |
|---|---|---|---|---|---|---|---|
| Wages at £ 3. 0. 0. per month, for Three Months _____ days | 9 | 18 | | * Reduction of Wages on disrating by £_____ per month for _____ months _____ days | | | |
| *Increase of wages on promotion by £_____ per month for _____ months _____ days. | | | | Advance on joining | 2 | | |
| | 3 | 6 | ½ | Allotments | | | |
| Overtime _____ Hours at_____ | | | | Fines | | | |
| | | | | Forfeitures | | | |
| | 10 | 1 | 6½ | Cash | 2 | 10 | 11 |
| | | | | Tobacco | | 4 | 2 |
| | | | | Slops | | | |
| | | | | Channel Money | | | |
| | | | | Insurance 1 Weeks Health & Pensions | | 1 | 6 |
| Deductions as per Contra .. | 5 | 15 | 4 | Unemployment | | | |
| Balance due .. £ | 4 | 5 | 11½ | Total Deductions .. £ | 5 | 15 | 4 |

Dated at the Port of____LONDON____

this __14__ day of____November____ 19 37.

W. G. Summers. { Signature of Master.

[TURN OVER.

I had just turned 17 when on the 16th August 1937, carrying my heavy kitbag over my shoulder, I climbed aboard the ship which was tied up in the London docks. She was the largest vessel of the fleet, but was later superseded by the newly built "Dominion Monarch" 27,155 tons. The "Monarch" then became the largest passenger/cargo liner to be regularly engaged on the UK to New Zealand route. During the 1939-45 war, she was converted and mainly used as a troop carrier. I was later surprised to learn my Uncle Mick had been appointed Bosun. Sadly, after my failure to rejoin the "Largs Bay", for no apparent reason, I never saw or spoke to him again.

The round trip totalled three months and nine days. My wages for the whole voyage including overtime, came to £10-1-6½ (£10.08). After a stoppage of 14 weeks insurance amounting to 17/6 (87p), I was left with £9-4-0½, (£9.21). I thought it well worth it though, watching fascinated as we negotiated the intricate locks of the Panama canal. I had observed the beautiful green scenery as we steamed slowly and serenely through the still waters; a stark contrast to the journey through most areas of the Suez canal, with its accompanying sandy stretches of desert.

By the time I returned to London, I'd travelled round the world and had achieved my ambition. I decided it would be advantageous to settle down and obtain regular employment. At the same time, I embarked on a course to become a member of the Civil Service as a Customs and

Excise Officer. I fancied I would still be involved with ships in that position. Unfortunately, after two years of constant studying, Adolph Hitler put paid to my aspirations. All interviews and tests were cancelled for the duration of the war. By the time the conflict ended, I was over 25. Being a few months above the qualifying age limit, it precluded me from sitting the preliminary examination.

During the next two years, I was employed by Grocers J. Sainsbury, at a small retail outlet in Barking, Essex. Large supermarkets were unheard of in those days. Hundredweight casks of Danish butter would be cut, then patted into ½ or 1 lb. blocks with crude wooden instruments. Customers waited patiently for their individual orders to be wrapped. All cooked meats, including ham, ox tongue, corned beef, brawn, liver sausage etc., were also sliced and wrapped by hand. Huge cheeses were cut to requirements with the aid of a length of wire.

On a Saturday afternoon a young assistant would stand outside on the pavement holding aloft a pig's head. He would shout loudly, "Who wants one for a shilling?" (5p). Thirty-six Polish eggs would cost the same amount. To ensure that the eggs were fresh, each one was meticulously candled by a staff member. The method was rather crude, holding the egg against a light bulb encased in a metal holder. However, it indicated if an egg was bad. Cracked eggs could be purchased very cheaply.

Sainsbury were very strict with their employees' appearance. Our fingernails were inspected each morning. A white jacket, white apron, tie and black polished shoes were the order of the day. Staff jackets had black buttons, while First Hands (under managers) were distinguished by having red buttons. Even before the war, the Company was widely known for cleanliness and the quality of their food.

On one occasion the Manager, Mr. James, asked if I would like to paint a large sign at the rear of the shop, using my own discretion. On his instructions, I painted in large black capital letters the following sentence, "Let no man say that this place was untidy before he came". When I had finished he said, "Well done, I knew that if anyone could do it, it would be you". For some reason, this incident, like so many others, is forever embedded in my memory. There was little sign of the war ending and I began to get restless, worrying whether I should join the armed forces. My younger brother Bill had already joined the Navy as an A.B (Able bodied seaman). He was serving overseas on a destroyer, HMS "Gallant". After giving the matter a great deal of thought, I decided to "play my part" and volunteered to rejoin the Merchant Navy.

My mother naturally did not approve, but I nevertheless resigned my job and made my way to the docks. After going through the preliminaries at the Shipping Federation and the Mercantile Marine office in Connaught Rd, there was a cursory medical examination by the Federation

GALLANT

Doctor and I was pronounced fit. I was accepted for service, but it seemed I must do one more trip before being upgraded to the rank of Ordinary Seaman. Being only nineteen at the time, I didn't have much choice, although my duties were the same as an O.S. These included a two hour stint at the helm, with another two hours spent on look-out in the crow's nest. This duty was to become an important factor in my life, as with the events that unfolded, this determined my fate. The interview at the M.o.D. was soon concluded and I was informed that I would be notified of my next voyage within a few days.

Having my discharge book as identification, I decided to have a look round the docks. As I walked through the open gates, guarded by one solitary unarmed policeman, a feeling of excitement came over me. Gazing around, seeing large sturdy ships in dock, I imagined myself on board again. I visualised rough, stormy open seas and could almost taste the salty spray as I pictured giant waves splashing over the dipping bow. I yearned to visit my home in Australia again, hoping it could be arranged. With a war in progress, it was not for me to decide, although I had stated my preference for Australia.

Within a few days I received orders to travel to Glasgow in Scotland. On arrival, I would join the S. S. "Turakina", owned by the New Zealand Shipping Company.

To date there have been five ships named "Turakina". It is the name of a small river in Taranaki, New Zealand

and in the Maori language means "fallen tree". The first "Turakina" was a sailing vessel of 1,247 tons, built in 1868, by Charles Connell of Glasgow and named "City of Perth". It was later sold to the New Zealand Shipping Company in 1882, and renamed "Turakina". It was then resold in 1889 to Tvedestrand, Norway and given a new name, "Elida".

The second "Turakina", with a gross tonnage of 9,920 tons, was built by Hawthorn Leslie and Co. Ltd of Newcastle England, in August 1902. On August 13th, 1918, during the 1914-1918 first World War, she was attacked by a German submarine. A torpedo was fired and she sank 120 miles W.S.W. from Bishops Rock and the Isle of Scilly. Two crew members were killed in that action.

The third ship was completed in September 1923 by William Hamilton and Co. Ltd. of Glasgow, Scotland, having a gross tonnage of 9,691 tons. With a single screw, she was capable of a top speed of 15 knots. On my joining this latest "Turakina", it proved to be the beginning of an incredible story. An unforgettable, frightening experience that would spread over 16 months.

On the 22nd April 1940, five eager, adventurous young men in their early twenties joined me at the busy Victoria station in London for the long tedious train journey north. Jack Abercrombie, an ordinary seaman (uncertified ) from East Ham, London, produced a pack of cards to help pass the long tedious hours away. Of the six carefree happy youths enjoying a little gamble, only three would live to make the return journey. Three would be killed in battle, while another would spend four long years in a prison camp in Germany.

# CHAPTER 3

## "THERE'S A BLOODY WAR ON"

I eventually joined the crew at Gourock, Scotland, with the S. S. "Turakina" preparing to sail. She was a typical cargo vessel, with black painted hull and a single beige funnel. I couldn't help noticing the 4.7" gun on the poop deck, not dreaming of its later significance. A Marine gunner would be in charge, helped by crew members. In those days, the food and accommodation for seamen left a lot to be desired. At sea, sixty-four hours was the basic working week. When on watch, it was usually four hours on and four hours off. When the ship tied up in dock, we would revert to daywork. One man would guard the gangway, while shore leave was available for most of the remainder.

Breakfast each morning meant dried apricots or prunes, whilst the midday meal was invariably stew. Every evening, a large tray of sliced cold beetroot and onion rings, loosely described as salad, was on offer. Sometimes, there would be a small slice of corned beef. Fruit was unavailable, unless we purchased our own when in port. On one occasion, I obtained a hand of very green bananas, hanging it securely above my bunk. It lasted for almost three weeks.

Different trades and ranks would dine and be accommodated separately. Seamen had their own mess room, while the Bosun and carpenter each occupied a small cabin. Also segregated were firemen, greasers, officers and stewards, each having their own quarters and dining arrangements. The deck boy would usually collect the Able and Ordinary Seamens' meals from the galley, although the O.S. normally assisted. The "Turakina" was alleged to be a hungry ship, but it was probably no worse than many others.

The Seamens' accommodation was directly below the fo'c'sle head, in the very bow of the ship. Our sleeping arrangements consisted of a dozen bunk beds with solid metal frames, built in two tiers. These were securely fixed around the perimeter and with each person possessing their own locker, conditions were considerably cramped.

It was the 23rd April 1940, when we finally sailed from the Mersey, bound for Australia, via the United States of America. I was amazed at the number of ships assembled, waiting for the order to depart. We had joined a large convoy and were soon on our way. It was an impressive sight seeing so many ships sailing together, although spaced widely apart. Being in large numbers, it gave us a feeling of confidence and safety. Looking around, I couldn't see any warships, but I assumed there must be a Naval escort, surface or otherwise.

Some time later, the "Turakina" actually parted from the convoy and proceeded to cross the Northern Atlantic alone. After a few days, we reached the east coast of America without incident. However, during the crossing, we heard rumours that the ship had developed a fault with her propeller. The result was a stay in dry dock in the port of Baltimore. After some delay, whatever the problem was, it was soon attended to.

We sailed north again to our next port of call, the busy city of Philadelphia. Here we loaded general cargo destined for New Zealand and Australia. On completion, we headed northwards again, docking in the capital, New York. It was a wonderful experience being so close to the impressive Statue of Liberty and seeing the towering skyscrapers for the first time. At night, the city was a fantastic blaze of light, a stark contrast to the total blackout home in Britain. I thought being in the Merchant Navy had its advantages - I could travel almost anywhere in the world and get paid for the experience. I liked the life, and wondered if I should train to become an officer.

It was the heyday of the beautiful passenger vessels of the Cunard Company. Among the large ships on the crossing were the "Queen Mary", "Empress of Britain", "Aquitania", "Lucitania" and the "Mauritania". They provided a regular service from Southampton to New

QUEEN MARY 1937

CAPT. J. LAIRD — SEATED CENTRE 1938

ss "TURAKINA" V.31- Sailed from Liverpool for Australia 12th. Nov. 1938

York. The cost was far above the average persons means, for cheap air travel and package tours were non-existent at that time.

Additional cargo was taken aboard and we were soon sailing southwards along the east coast. The scenic Panama canal was negotiated and we sailed serenely for Brisbane, the capital city of Queensland, the north-eastern State of Australia. I was looking forward to reaching my home town of Melbourne again. During the long monotonous journey across the Pacific, there was little constructive work done. Time was spent on the two hour lookout in the crow's nest or on the fo'c'sle head, depending on the weather conditions. Otherwise, it would be chipping and painting handrails or a further two hour stint taking the wheel. At times, wearing traditional sea-boots, us younger men most days would scrub the wooden decks with buckets of sea water and a hard broom. On one occasion, Captain Laird stood on the bridge and shouted, "Put your backs into it, you bloody army dodgers!".

A few days later, in the Pacific Ocean, I was on afternoon watch with my two hour stretch at the helm. Suffering with a very bad cold, I'd had very little sleep the previous night due to a dry cough. I was tired and on my own at the time. With my arms outstretched holding the steering wheel, I leaned backwards against the chart room. Unfortunately I must have dropped off to sleep for some seconds. Because of having to steer manually and the waves striking the port bow, the "Turakina" was steering a circular course. I was awakened by a loud bellow from the Captain, "What's up man, don't you know there's a bloody war on!". I said meekly, "Sorry Captain" and explained my problem. I was cautioned never to repeat the incident, and in future, to report sick when not well.

We continued on our designated course without further incident, and we travelled round the Australian coast, unloading and loading at the various State capitals. Our final port of call in Australia would be Sydney, before crossing the Tasman Sea, bound for Wellington, New Zealand. After so many weeks at sea, although still enjoying the life, plus a wonderful time spent in Australia, I was looking forward to the long haul back to my family in England.

# CHAPTER 4

## A BATTLE IN THE TASMAN SEA

The toss of a coin proved to be a most significant moment in my life. In the events that followed, the result of that coin toss no doubt determined who would live or die. On the evening of the 20th August, Ordinary Seaman Sydney Manders and I were due on duty between 4 and 8 p.m. In seaman's terms, it was known as the "dog watch". With the ship pitching and rolling violently in the rough seas, accompanied by heavy rain and howling winds, being up the foremast on lookout was not a pleasant task to undertake.

Although paid deck boy rates, my duties were the same as for ordinary seamen. Sydney and I agreed on the heads or tails solution to decide who would take first watch. It meant ascending the foremast and climbing into the crow's nest for the two hour stint. On the toss of that coin, the fates declared it to be Sydney. The alternative duty was of stand-by on the bridge. I would relieve my shipmate at 6pm, reversing our roles. Against the howling winds, I battled my way to the bridge and stood in a sheltered position on the port side, awaiting orders. I had a clear view of the surrounding raging seas. Peering into the wheelhouse, I could see the helmsman and the Chief Officer, Mr. Neagle.

It was about 4.30 p.m. when I first noticed the German vessel in the distance, a black sinister shape appearing through the mist and showery downpours of heavy rain. I watched curiously as she approached on our port bow, then swung round to our starboard side. I thought it rather unusual, but nobody imagined a German raider would be operating in the Tasman Sea. The marauder then rounded our stern, reaching a position on our port beam. These manoeuvres were carried out in an endeavour to bar our escape route to Cook Strait, New Zealand.

Between the intermittent showery squalls, the "Orion", or the "Black Raider", as she became known, would disappear from view, reappearing again in the far away mist. From my position on the bridge, I noticed the Chief Officer had been joined by Captain Laird. They were in deep conversation, no doubt discussing the situation and deciding on our next move.

The Captain was very distinguished looking. A strict, thick set, tall man, with close cropped greyish hair and bushy eyebrows, it was widely known he had vowed to fight back if ever attacked. At the helm was Able Seaman Gorman, while the ship's telephone was attended by a young apprentice Officer, Alistair Taylor, on his very first voyage.

In the storm lashed seas, the "Orion" was gradually closing in on her prey, trying to gain a more advantageous position. I could see the flashing of Morse signals as the German Captain Weyher indicated, "Do not use your radio". This order was ignored by Captain Laird. Our radio officers continued to transmit radio signals indicating the impending attack. Our approximate position was given as 400 miles from Wellington and 200 miles from Cape Egmont, off the coast of the southern island of New Zealand.

Above the noise of the prevailing stormy winds, I heard the blaring sound of action stations. There was a hasty but orderly rush of men attending their allotted positions. I was running down below to collect my life jacket when I heard the first salvo fired by the enemy. Hastily donning the jacket, I ran swiftly up on deck. There was another loud deafening blast as our gun crew fired their first shell.

It was a few minutes before 6 p.m. when I reported back to the bridge, that being my station during an emergency. The enemy gunners were now finding their range, although experiencing some difficulty in holding their target. This was due to the excessive rolling and pitching of their vessel in the mountainous seas. A prolonged, relentless barrage began, with some shells finding their target. I could plainly hear them as they whined and whistled overhead. I stood at my station and watched as shells splashed into the sea alongside both our port and starboard sides.  Visibility was becoming poor as the darkness approached, with ominous black clouds forming overhead.

The "Orion" was a formidable adversary, equipped with a main battery of six 5.9 inch guns and a twin barrelled anti-aircraft gun.  In addition there were six 21" torpedo tubes.  Also aboard was an Arado seaplane, used mainly during fine weather, when a search was made for unwary Allied ships. We were hopelessly outclassed in fire-power, the only means of defence the 4.7 inch gun mounted on the after deck.  The Marine gunner was in command of the gunnery crew.  The weather worsened with angry seas and strong winds howling as if to compete with the whining of the shells.  On board there was calm, with no panic or confusion.  As the onslaught continued, the upper foremast received a direct hit.  It was sent crashing onto the deck, bouncing overboard into the raging seas along with the lookout, Sidney Manders.

The aerial was destroyed, cancelling out further signals by the two radio officers, S. K. Jones and J. W. Penny. Shortly afterwards, another deadly shell burst into the wireless room.  Both operators died during the action. The Lloyds War Medal is the highest award that can be made to British seamen.  This was later awarded posthumously to the Chief Radio Officer, S. K. Jones. From my position on the bridge, I noticed A.B.Gorman still standing calmly at the wheel as the Captain and Chief Officer left the bridge.  I could see small fires had already started amidships. The Chief Officer ordered fire stations and being on standby, I said, "What can I do?". He replied, "You had better give the gun crew a hand". In the turmoil of the action, I hurriedly made my way aft and, along with Frank Quinn, assisted in unpacking and passing the heavy shells to other members of the ammunition column. The enemy's savage bombardment showed no signs of easing.

I heard another loud explosion when a shell crashed and burst into the bridge, killing the helmsman, A.B. Gorman. Almost immediately, another shell crashed into the Cadets' house, while further shells hurtled into the Engineers' quarters and the galley, which was situated close to the funnel. The engine room was also hit, killing the 5th Engineer and three other crew members. It wasn't long before greedy flames began to spread angrily, engulfing the areas that were alight. The fire was becoming so fierce that the Chief Officer ordered most of the members of the ammunition column, including myself, to assist the 2nd. Officer, Mr. Hudson, in fighting the fires. This resulted in our gun becoming silent for a short space of time. Believing we had surrendered, the "Orion" ceased firing and began to close in to pick up survivors.

# ABANDON SHIP

I saw Captain Laird leave his cabin carrying a canvas bag and I noticed his face was bleeding. Realising our gun was silent, he shouted , "Keep firing at the *******!". By now, the gun crew were very short-handed due to fire fighting. The fires were increasing in their ferocity, so the Captain, coming to terms with the futility of the situation, yelled loudly, "Take to the lifeboats!". He then signalled with a long and loud blast to abandon ship.

It must have been almost simultaneously that our depleted gun crew managed to open fire again, to the consternation of the Germans, who were about to carry out rescue operations. Evidently, the remainder of our gun crew had not heard the "abandon ship" signal. The enemy immediately replied with further salvos, increasing their fire-power with the use of their twin barrelled anti-aircraft gun. The latter repeatedly fired tracer shells.

By this time, I could see the "Turakina" was well ablaze. Colourful flames reached out like giant Roman candles, lighting up the darkened skies. As I and other crew members made our way to the lifeboats another shell hit the funnel. A flying piece of shrapnel struck my forehead.

Luckily, it caused only a slight wound and soon stopped bleeding. There were four lifeboats aboard, but two on the port side were unserviceable with the davits all buckled and bent. They had been too badly damaged to be of use. Fortunately, the starboard boats were in good order.

Fourth Officer Spencer was in charge of the aft boat. It was lowered a short distance while some of the survivors clambered aboard. Hanging from the davits, the boat swung and smashed repeatedly against the hull with terrific force due to the excessive rolling of the ship in the turbulent seas. It was a harrowing experience. I thought the lifeboat would break up, the pounding was so severe. In the furore of the moment, along with other crew members, I jumped into the boat as it was launched. It was immediately swept away, finishing up under the stern. The "Turakina" was still moving forward very slowly, settling a little lower in the water. There had been no time to grab the oars. In our situation, a lifeboat with an engine would have been a godsend. Nevertheless, I and a few others eventually managed to ship the oars, but we found it very difficult to row in the sea conditions.

The lifeboat was tossed about like a cork, one moment in a deep trough and the next on top of the white crest of a huge wave. Consequently, we were drifting further away from our vessel. Well alight and silhouetted against the darkened skies, the stricken ship rather wearily moved forward in the heavy seas. The German Captain decided to hasten her destruction by using his precious torpedoes.

One was dispatched, but did little damage as it failed to hit below the water line. A few seconds later, another torpedo was fired, this time finding its target. I saw a flash, and almost simultaneously, it was followed by a terrific explosion. It lit up the surrounding area for a few seconds.

I saw huge lumps of metal and debris flying high into the sky, spreading out over a wide area, then splashing down into the sea. Some large chunks fell alarmingly close to the lifeboat. I watched in horror as, in a very short space of time, the "Turakina", stern first, began to slowly slip into the sea. Towards the end, she seemed to gather speed, going down quite fast as she disappeared below the surface. Suddenly all was quiet and peaceful. There was an eerie silence. A very sad, dramatic moment in time, etched in my mind.

These events, combined with bitterly cold winds, had taken their toll. I was soaking wet from the spray and felt very tired. My whole body shook, my teeth chattered as the pitch black darkness of the night took over once more. In the mountainous sea, the lifeboat was riding the waves efficiently. One moment rising to a great height on the crest of a wave, then falling quickly and disappearing from view. It felt like a roller coaster.

Suddenly, somebody shouted, "Look over there!". As I peered into the gloom, in the dark shadows I saw three of our fellow crew members desperately swimming and struggling in a effort to reach the lifeboat. Reaching out with arms outstretched, the survivors were eventually grabbed and hauled into the boat. One of the men was the lookout, Sydney Manders. I could see he was severely wounded, with terrible injuries to his face and body. He was still conscious, but unable to communicate. He was made as comfortable as possible under the extreme conditions.

There was a general feeling of exhaustion and disbelief in the aftermath of the action. We sat still as the lifeboat was allowed to drift. I now realise we must have been in a state of shock. I could hardly believe what had happened. In the total darkness, it was impossible to locate any more of our crew in the surrounding violent seas. The Germans however, could be seen in the distance, using their searchlight in an effort to locate and rescue any further survivors.

We had not been seen by the enemy and there was a difference of opinion between the Officer in charge and some of our crew. He firmly believed our attacker was a British vessel that had made a mistake. This could have been feasible, as it was not known or even imagined by the Allies that enemy ships would be operating so close to Australia and New Zealand. Some men wanted to try to reach New Zealand, while others argued that there was a possibility of being found by search parties. After some discussion, and bearing in mind there was a dying man on board, it was agreed to signal the Germans. The Officer did so by flashing the "Orion" with a torch from the lifeboat.

Due to the heavy seas, a rescue boat could not be launched. On Captain Weyher's orders, the cruiser moved slowly and carefully until they were alongside. A Jacob's ladder was quickly thrown overboard. It fell to where I was sitting and as I grabbed hold, Officer Spencer shouted, "Up you go!". I was the first to negotiate the tricky and hazardous climb aboard. It was very difficult owing to the rise and fall of the lifeboat, coupled with the buffeting of the German vessel. As I precariously climbed the ladder, I had mixed feelings. I was apprehensive and rather scared. I also had a sense of great relief at leaving the heaving lifeboat. But, being the first one to climb aboard, I wondered what kind of reception awaited. Would I be beaten up in reprisal for our fight-back? Looking up, I saw two burly German sailors leaning over the ship's side waiting to grab me.

On reaching the top, I was put at ease as they hauled me over, gently depositing me on the deck. While doing so, one said in English, "Are you OK?". Still unsure of their attitude, I was reassured when I was immediately handed a mug of hot tea. It was the finest tea I have ever tasted. It wasn't long before the remaining crew from the lifeboat were taken on board. The badly injured Sydney Manders was stretchered and taken to the hospital. A young German Officer approached and said, "You were good shots, with plenty of near misses". It was then that I noticed the damage to the dummy deck house, the result of the one successful hit by our gun crew. The Germans evidently suffered some minor casualties of their own in the incident, and they were also being treated in the hospital.

My blood-stained forehead was later cleaned and dressed with a small plaster, but I had no further complications. It wasn't too long before we were issued with blankets and escorted below into one of the holds. This was our living and sleeping accommodation for the many weeks to follow. Although feeling exhausted, I had a fretful time for most of the night, lying awake and reliving the ordeal of the earlier traumatic hours. I thought of my home and family, and of the men who must have died during the conflict.

We were battened down below with no means of escape. This was the normal procedure for most of the time, particularly when the klaxon horn sounded action stations. I'd hardly dozed off, when we were aroused and greeted with ersatz black coffee. Not very nice, but at least it was hot. We were later allowed up on deck to meet our surviving Officers who were imprisoned in their own quarters elsewhere.

# CHAPTER 5

## LIFE ON AN ENEMY RAIDER

Third Officer J. R. Mallett confirmed the details of the events of the previous day. We were informed of the sad news that the Captain, Chief Officer, Chief Engineer, Second Engineer and several others were standing near No. 5 hatch when, without warning, a second torpedo struck. Most of these men were never seen again. The force of the explosion wrecked the second lifeboat, with only eight men surviving. Sydney Manders did not recover from his injuries, despite the best efforts of the German medical staff to save him.

The German Captain slowly edged the "Orion" closer to the scene of the actual sinking. With the aid of a powerful searchlight, he combed the area for five hours, searching for further survivors. He did this in spite of knowing that the Australian and New Zealand stations had received our radio signals, giving the approximate position of the attack. Their radio officer had picked up signals from Brisbane in Queensland, Australia, indicating the "Turakina's" plight. It has been recorded, that Capt. Weyher probably ordered the search to ensure that all survivors would be rescued to prevent valuable information relating to the raider being disclosed to the Allied forces. It may have been true, but in my personal opinion, I believe it was done for humanitarian reasons. Weyher, who in his early days had served as a Commander of a submarine, even praised the spirited action of our gun crew. But he also declared that we were "mad Britishers" for fighting against such overwhelming odds.

As the seas were running so high, the Germans had been unable to launch their own lifeboats in their rescue attempts. Instead, small rubber boats were used to aid in the search. Amongst those taken from the water were the two young men, apprentice Alistair Taylor, and Seventh Engineer, Allan Slater. In the aftermath of the battle, we learned the extent of our casualties. In total our crew numbered fifty-seven. Of those, thirty-six men lost their lives, while twenty-one were taken prisoners-of-war. I came to the conclusion that our future was rather uncertain, to say the least. I thought our chances of survival on the raider were minimal, knowing the strength of the Allied Navies.

There was no doubt that Captain Weyher, like Captain Laird, would also fight against superior forces if the situation arose. The possibilities were discussed over and over again. We could only conjecture as to our fate and prayed we would live to tell the tale. I later spoke with a guard, who admitted they were unhappy with their Captain's decision to create a five hour delay in making their escape from the area. Their misgivings had been the same as ours. Our position was made plain when, on another occasion, one said bluntly, "If we go down, then so will you!"

Berthed at Wellington, was the New Zealand cruiser, HMNZS "Achilles". Urgently made ready, she soon set sail at full speed, heading for the Tasman Sea. With a speed of about 25 knots, she would probably reach the scene by the following morning. Some hours later, a seaplane took off from New Zealand to aid in the search. Also, an Australian warship, HMAS "Perth", left Melbourne and accompanied by aircraft, covered the south-western areas of the Tasman Sea. At approximately the same time that the "Orion" made the final search for survivors, both warships had left their respective ports, heading for the area. During the hunt, the weather worsened considerably, with visibility becoming poor. Dense black clouds, heavy rain and the rough seas all increased in intensity.

The appalling conditions were very much in favour of the "Black Raider" and her crew. Combined with the darkness of the night, it enabled them to avoid detection. In daylight, the only sign to be seen of the action was a huge trailing oil slick, many miles in length. The following day, we were permitted on deck to attend the burial of Sydney Manders. I couldn't help thinking that, but for the toss of that coin, it would have been me. The service was conducted by Capt. Weyher and was also attended by some of his crew. As he was committed to the sea, covered with a Union Jack, the Germans sang in their own language, "I had a good comrade".

After four days being tossed about in the stormy seas, we rounded Tasmania, the southern tip of Australia, and traversed the Australian Bight. The plan was to keep within sight of the shipping lanes and intercept further victims. None were sighted. The weather deteriorated even more, with the raider listing badly from side to side as she battled her way through the notorious rough seas of the Bight. On the 2nd September, two dummy and two genuine mines were laid on the approaches to Albany, Western Australia. We heard later, one live mine was mishandled and had exploded on board. One crew member was severely wounded and died the following day, while a number of others were severely injured.

On September 3rd, action stations sounded. We were immediately battened and locked down below. We voiced our worries. Would we be bombed by Allied planes? Maybe we would be attacked by our own naval ships. A third alternative was that another unfortunate merchant vessel was about to be attacked. We could only nervously conjecture to the outcome. It transpired that a Hudson bomber plane had flown directly overhead. Some of the German crew hurriedly ran on deck wearing civilian clothes and waved their arms in greeting. The plane circled low overhead a few times and then flew off, much to the relief of the Germans. Other planes were searching in the vicinity, but all failed to detect or suspect the "Orion". Eventually, all reported back to their base at

Busselton, Western Australia. One of our guards thought it was hilarious when he later mentioned the incident, but I am sure it wasn't funny at the time.

The raider rounded the south-western coast and entered the Indian Ocean. They hunted for victims along the normal sea routes without success. On September 9th, Capt. Weyher received orders to return to the Pacific Ocean. In the meantime, we were being allowed on deck for an hour each day, when weather and circumstances permitted. On one occasion I was astonished to see a number of the crew, busily engaged in a repainting job. I watched in amazement as brown paint was hurriedly slapped over the upper white parts of the ship. False deck houses were moved and the dummy gun prominently displayed aft. The "Orion" was undergoing a transformation into a new disguise. In a short space of time we had become a British merchant vessel, with a new name painted on the hull.

There was little improvement in the freezing cold stormy weather as we again crossed the Bight, this time in an easterly direction. Continuously buffeted by heavy seas, we skirted around Tasmania and re-entered the Tasman Sea. The northern and southern areas were patrolled for several days, but no ships were sighted. Six weeks had passed since the "Turakina" was sunk and the Germans had not achieved any further successes. Owing to a shortage of oil and stores, an arrangement had been made for a meeting with a supply ship in the vicinity of the Marshall Islands.

Our rendezvous was the atoll of Ailinglapalap, just north of the Equator. We sailed northwards, with the weather gradually improving as each day passed. Eventually, we crossed the Equator and our conditions below became unbearable. Instead of freezing cold, our hold became like an oven. We were stifled by the heat and there was precious little fresh air. Sometimes, when it rained, we were allowed on deck for a nice refreshing shower, although soap was a very scarce commodity. Ever watchful armed guards were always in attendance on these occasions.

On October 10th, there was a commotion on deck and I heard the sound of running feet overhead. The engines stopped. Suddenly, it became very quiet as the "Orion" glided slowly and silently through the calm water. Then came the noisy rattle of the anchor as it dropped into the sea. What was going on? We didn't know the answer. We were unaware of the proposed meeting with the German supply ship "Regensberg". She sailed under the Japanese flag as the "Tokyo Maru". Both ships came alongside and were roped together. Over the next two days oil was pumped aboard the "Orion" and stores were replenished. With the ship at a standstill, the heat was even more oppressive, and the sweat just dripped from my body.

On October 12th "Orion" upped anchor. Not being allowed up on deck during the last two days, it was a great relief being on the move. It allowed much needed extra ventilation. There was now some discussion and conjecture amongst us, wondering what might be taking place. There was no news of our destination. Occasionally, snippets of information filtered through. We would learn of previous events concerning the raider's movements. When, questioned about future plans for us, they had no idea. Our fate was in the lap of the gods, as well as Adolph Hitler. Regarding the war, there was no information, not even German propaganda.

The "Orion" was now masquerading as a Japanese vessel. I watched as a new name was painted on the sides. It was the "Maebasi Maru". I had been a prisoner for fifty-three tedious, boring days without seeing land, but I felt fortunate to be alive. We talked mainly of our families and friends, likes and dislikes, hobbies, being back home and the war. After a time, these topics had become exhausted and there was little conversation. Some men tended to keep to themselves, alone with their thoughts. It was probably due to boredom, worry or a combination of them. Boredom was the biggest problem, as there was no radio, books or literature of any description.

There were playing cards though, and I played practically all day long. Our daily diet, although nothing fancy, was adequate. It was black ersatz coffee for breakfast, with two meals later. For lunch it was soup and the evening meal, a chunk of dry black bread with a chunk of German sausage. The bread seemed horrible at first but, after a time, I became accustomed to the taste and really enjoyed it.

The "Orion", accompanied by the "Regensberg", still keeping her guise as the "Tokyo Maru", reached the East Caroline Islands. Quite close to the Equator, it was steaming hot and humid. In the early hours of October 14th we were suddenly awakened by the loud blaring sound of action stations. Our hatch was immediately battened down. The gun and magazines were located very close to our hold and I heard the unmistakable sound of the mounting of the gun. Shortly afterwards, there was an indescribably loud explosion immediately above us, as a shell was fired. Due to the hollowness of our quarters and the close proximity of the gun, the noise reverberated intensely and we were terrified by this sudden unexpected shock to our senses.

I put my fingers in my ears as a second blast occurred. Locked securely down below, I anxiously awaited further developments. There was great relief all round, when the silence remained unbroken. It left us in a state of suspense. What was going on? We were to find out very shortly. A Norwegian ship, the "Ringwood" 7,203 tons, was on her way to Ocean Island in the Pacific when she unfortunately encountered the "Orion". The first shell was dispatched across her bow. The warning to stop went unheeded by Captain Parker, the Master of the "Ringwood". The second shot fired was a close miss, so the Captain gave the order to stop engines.

As the vessel came slowly to a standstill, a number of armed Germans clambered aboard. Thirty-six men, including four Chinese, were taken prisoner. They were transferred to the "Orion", along with a large quantity of stores. Once his needs were satisfied, Captain Weyher decided to sink the captive ship. Without further delay, the "Ringwood" was scuttled and disappeared without trace.

The Norwegian crew, with the exception of the Officers and the Chinese, were ushered into our quarters. The latter were segregated from the rest, imprisoned in the "coloured" accommodation elsewhere. On meeting the Norwegians, we could hardly say, "Welcome aboard. It's good to see you!". However, it was a pleasant change to see some new faces. The language was not a problem as most could speak English. It was almost two months since we'd had news of the outside world. We were told London was being bombed daily by the German Air Force. It was the beginning of the Blitz, leading up to the Battle of Britain. It was during that time that the Spitfire and Hurricane fighter planes played their noble part in the defeat of the Luftwaffe. We also learned that Germany, Italy and Japan had signed a ten year pact in Berlin. I came to the conclusion there was some truth in the saying, "No news is good news".

The Norwegians thoughtfully brought more playing cards and draughts. I was pleased with the latter as I considered myself a good player. At last there was something else to occupy our minds. The games certainly helped to pass away the long tedious hours, as well as giving our brains much needed exercise.

Someone suggested we play draughts for slices of sausage. However, as I remained undefeated, the games for sausage were soon abandoned. Another luxury they managed to bring aboard were large cartons of Camel and Lucky Strike. These American cigarettes were like gold dust. To their credit, the Norwegians occasionally handed them around, a welcome addition to our ten per week ration of a Russian variety. The Russian tobacco was black in colour and so strong it was almost impossible to inhale without choking.

Over the next four days it remained quiet and peaceful with no further incidents. The two German ships reached the Lamotrek atoll in the Caroline Islands. They were joined by a second raider, the "Komet", a small vessel of 3,250 tons. Notwithstanding, she was well armed and equipped with ten torpedo tubes, six 5.9" guns, anti-aircraft guns and, like the "Orion", possessed an Arado seaplane. She was accompanied by another German supply ship, the "Kulmerland", an unarmed vessel.

There were now four German vessels at the previously arranged meeting. The object was to carry out necessary repairs to the raiders, supplying various essential commodities including oil, food and clothing. During these operations, we were not allowed on deck. On October 20th, as the "Regensburg's" supplies had become exhausted, she left the atoll and sailed for Japan. A few days later she reached her destination without incident. In the meantime, the two raiders and their supply ships sailed from the area, having arranged to operate together.

Over the previous four days, with the "Orion" lying perfectly still, we had endured overwhelming oppressive heat and were pleased to be moving again. The German ships were now all sailing under the Japanese flag. The "Kulmerland" was the "Tokyo Maru", the "Orion" still the "Maebesi Maru", whilst the "Komet" became the "Manyo Maru". Their orders were to cover the busy routes used by passenger and cargo vessels travelling from New Zealand. The majority of these ships would be heading for the British Isles, via the Panama Canal.

The "Kulmerland" was a fairly large ship of about 9,000 tons. While they searched for further victims, she was escorted by the raiders, one on either side. They travelled many miles apart in order to patrol as wide an area as possible. However, for many weeks they operated their combined exercises without success.

Although I was glad to be alive, life down below had become very humdrum. The monotony was often relieved by the many terrific storms that we encountered. Some lasted four or five days before abating, with the "Orion" on many occasions seeming about to capsize. I thought I was quite a good sailor, never becoming seasick, but I have never experienced a ship that rolled as alarmingly as the "Orion". It was terrifying, particularly during those violent storms. Sometimes, Weyher would slow the engines, with the ship moving very slowly. We would almost heave to and be tossed about amongst the giant waves, riding out the storm.

After we left the atoll; there was a welcome change to our diet. It was the introduction of tinned whalemeat, processed in Japan. It was an acquired taste. When the weather was calm, we could relax a little. Many hours continued to be spent playing card games and, my speciality, Draughts.

The Germans had combed the seas for thirty-six days when, early on the morning of November 25th, the dreaded action stations signal sounded. This was always a tense time, because we didn't know what was happening. I rather hoped we would not be intercepted by a superior Allied battleship. It would definitely be a fight to a finish with us battened down in the hold. Being next to the magazine didn't help to calm the nerves either.

In a situation parallel to ours, on May 8th 1941, the German armed raider "Pinguin" was attacked by HMS "Cornwall" in the Indian Ocean, north of Madagasca, off the islands of the Seychelles. Over two hundred captured British seamen who were imprisoned on the "Pinguin" lost their lives in the action. The German vessel had a crew totalling 420 men. Of these, only about sixty survived the battle.

After the "Orion's" alarm sounded, we waited expectantly for the deafening firing of the guns. However, to our relief, it remained silent. The raider "Komet", some distance away, had spotted a small steamer of 546 tons, the "Holmwood". She had sailed from the Chatham Islands bound for Lyttleton, New Zealand and was about 500 miles east of her destination when intercepted. On this occasion, the target did not come under gunfire.

Her Master, Captain Miller, had been concerned with the safety of his passengers, so he decided against using his radio. Twenty-nine prisoners, including four women and two children, were taken aboard the smaller "Komet". The capture of the "Holmwood" provided more stores and a number of live sheep. A German guard said they had a good time riding the sheep around the decks. Although the Germans had replenished their store supply, it made no difference as far as we were concerned. After three months on our monotonous diet, the thought of eating roast lamb with mint sauce was a tantalising fantasy.

Soon the "Holmwood" was scuttled by the Germans and finally sunk by gunnery practice from the "Komet".

Two days later, at about 3am, I was awakened from a deep sleep, again by the dreaded signal of action stations. Still tired and not fully awake, I waited with some trepidation for something to happen. After a few anxious minutes that seemed an eternity, the "Orion's" guns opened fire. As the barrage began, the noise was so frightening that a fair headed young Norwegian became panic stricken, rushed over to a ventilator and attempted to climb through and up on deck, but it was impossible for him to escape the deafening sounds of the gun, as the opening was much too small. He was quickly restrained by a couple of his shipmates. If he had succeeded in climbing up on deck, under the circumstances, I am sure it would have proved fatal. Later, I learned the reason for the relentless bombardment.

# THE SINKING OF THE RANGITANE

The "Rangitane" 16,712 tons, like the "Turakina", was owned by the New Zealand Shipping Company. A large combined passenger and refrigeration vessel, she was on her regular voyage from New Zealand to Great Britain. In command was Captain H. L. Upton, DS, RDRN. On board were about two hundred crew, and 111 passengers. Included in the total were thirty-six women. On November 23rd, the "Rangitane" sailed from Auckland and anchored off the mainland. She had just taken on board a consignment of butter, frozen meat, wool and general merchandise. The following day she upped anchor and embarked on her regular voyage to the United Kingdom. At about 3.45 am, the raiders were spotted by the "Rangitane". Her alarm bells rang out, awaking the passengers and off duty crew members.

The Germans transmitted Morse signals, ordering Captain Upton to stop. He ignored this demand, instead he ordered radio signals to be transmitted, indicating a suspicious ship. On picking up these signals, the "Orion" and "Komet" opened up with a ferocious barrage. It lasted for about twenty minutes. As a result, five crew members and five passengers were killed. There were

AUCKLAND 1937

91

also quite a number of wounded people, some with very severe injuries.

Captain Upton stopped his ship, after the radio messages had been sent. He then signalled the Germans that women and children were on board. As soon as this message was received, the "Orion" and "Komet" ceased their deadly crossfire. Shortly afterwards, armed Germans came aboard urging the survivors to hurry and take to the lifeboats. Most of these boats were speedily towed away by the German launches. All were taken prisoner aboard the German vessels and the injured were taken to the ships' hospitals for treatment. Needless to say, more precious food supplies from the "Rangitane" were confiscated. Unfortunately, it still made little difference to our staple diet.

Knowing Captain Upton's radio signals had been picked up, the German Captains were eager to make their getaway. The "Rangitane" was burning fiercely, but there was no sign of her sinking. To speed up the operation, the sea cocks were opened by crew members from the "Orion". The "Komet" then fired one lethal torpedo, which hit the target causing substantial damage. This was followed by more firing practice for the "Komet's" gunners. Soon afterwards the stricken ship disappeared beneath the waves, sinking to the bottom of the ocean.

The following day, the "Achilles" reached the scene of the action. An oil slick had spread over a large area, but little else was seen. Two flying boats, the "Aotearoa" and the

"Awarua" left Auckland to assist in the hunt for the raiders. Another vessel, the armed merchant ship "Puriri", also left New Zealand with orders to search the area. However, all efforts to locate the three German ships proved fruitless.

The enemy ships then set off, sailing at full speed to the north-east. They continued searching for further victims, travelling three abreast, again covering a wide area. That evening I heard the sound of the aircraft warning. A flying boat had been seen in the distance. The enemy were very fortunate and were not detected, due to the failing light. With darkness approaching, the pilot decided to continue his flight back to his Auckland base, to the great relief of the Germans. During the long dark nights, the three vessels would sail closer together.

On the 29th November, we reached the Kermadec Islands, some 960 kilometres north of Auckland. We hove to for a short time, while some prisoners were redistributed. Thirty-nine women and five children along with a number of other personnel, were transferred to the supply ship "Kulmerland". Conditions there were evidently more suitable. For the prisoners on the "Komet", the amenities were very good in comparison with the "Orion". They received ample reading material, while excellent meals were served by the "Rangitane's" stewards. Because of the extreme heat, they were issued with new navy shorts and white singlets. Music was relayed over loudspeakers, with regular news bulletins broadcast.

On the "Orion", we had none of these luxuries. Soap, food and cigarettes were always in short supply. However, I must admit we were always treated with respect, with no arrogance or animosity shown. Our sleeping arrangements in hammocks proved no hardship, in fact I found it quite comfortable. The gentle rocking of the ship, would soon send me to sleep.

Seven days later, action stations sounded, followed by the blast from the gun. Anxious moments passed, then came a deafening barrage from both the "Orion" and the "Komet". What would it mean on this occasion? Locked securely down below, none of us could be certain of the outcome.

# THE ISLAND OF NAURU

The "Triona", a small vessel of 4,413 tons, was owned by the British Phosphates Commission and had left Newcastle, Australia, bound for Nauru. She was a regular visitor to the remote Pacific island, situated approximately north-west of New Guinea. In effort to escape, she came under heavy fire from the two German raiders. It was a hopeless attempt, the "Triona" was soon forced to surrender.

As a result of the action, three crew members were killed, with sixty-eight survivors rescued, including six women passengers and one child. The "Kulmerland" and "Orion" shared the latest batch of prisoners between them. Once herded safely aboard and more stores appropriated, the "Triona" was torpedoed by the "Komet" and then sunk without trace.

In the early hours of the 8th December, we were awoken by the sound we'd come to dread. It was followed by the tumultuous sound of the guns as another target was attacked. After a few minutes, to the intense relief of all, the firing ceased. Hearing the throb of the engines, I knew it was full steam ahead. A few minutes passed, the engines slowed and the gunners recommenced their barrage.

Later, we learned from the guards that the "Orion" had intercepted two ships. The first was the "Triadic" 8,735 tons, also owned by the British Phosphate Commission. As a result of the shelling, she caught fire and the signal was given to abandon ship. The crew hastily took to their lifeboats. The "Orion" then gave chase to the second ship. It proved to be the "Triaster", 6,032 tons. It wasn't long before the "Orion's" broadsides found their target. The victim's lifeboats were launched and fifty-three prisoner taken on board.

The "Triaster" was finally sunk by explosive charges. She was the third vessel owned by the Commission to be attacked and destroyed, all within a few miles from Nauru. There was always a heavy traffic in the area, with the constant loading of phosphates from Nauru and Ocean Island. After ensuring there was no debris to be seen from the "Triaster", Captain Weyher turned his attention to the "Triadic", which he demolished with explosives and a torpedo.

Meanwhile, on the 7th December, the "Komet", commanded by Captain Robert Eyssen, had attacked the Norwegian vessel "Vinni", 5,181 tons. She was sunk using explosive charges, after the capture of thirty-two crew members. The following morning another unfortunate victim, the "Komata" 3,900 tons, owned by the Union Steamship Company, was heavily shelled until finally dispatched to the sea-bed.

Having achieved considerable success in sinking another five ships, the German Captains decided to sail together from the vicinity of Nauru and make good their escape. After an hour had passed without further shelling, I was able to relax again. The seas were running high, but I did not mind that. It was so quiet and peaceful, helping to soothe my frayed nerves.

The Germans were now confronted with a serious problem. The three ships were holding some 675 prisoners and were becoming overcrowded. There was a lack of suitable accommodation, combined with a shortage of food. The "Orion" alone had a complement of 377 men plus 265 detainees. Cooking for that amount was not an enviable task for those hands working in the heat of the kitchens, particularly when in the tropics.

Rumours had become rife concerning the fate of the prisoners. There was talk of us all being put ashore on one of the numerous lonely tropical islands dotted in the Pacific. My spirits rose as I pictured the scene. I visualised green trees, coconuts, luscious ripe juicy fruit hanging in bunches, white sandy beaches and calm blue seas. In my mind I imagined the waves gently breaking on the shores, with beautiful dusky skinned native girls dancing while wearing their long grass skirts. After four nerve-racking months confined on the "Orion", I couldn't believe it was true.

Our release would depend on signing the following agreement.

"We, the undersigned, do hereby give our word of honour and declare solemnly that, on our being set free, we will bear neither arms nor take military action against Germany or her Allies during the present hostilities. By breaching this agreement, we realise that we are liable to capital punishment". In the late afternoon of the 20th December, the three vessels hove to. The speculation began. I was feeling quite optimistic at the prospect of going ashore. The next morning I rose early, not being able to sleep, with my mind firmly fixed on my potential release.

As usual, we were locked down below, but could hear plenty of movement above. We were totally unaware of the happenings up on deck. Christmas Day would soon be upon us and a wonderful present could be in the offing. It would be great to see the back of the Jerries for the last time. There was a general feeling of expectancy and hope, rather than one of uncertainty and despair.

# UTOPIA FOR SOME

Emirau Island, also known as Storm Island, was once a German possession. It is situated in the Bismarck Archipelago to the north-east of New Guinea. A beautiful isle, it is surrounded by coral reefs and lagoons, encompassing an approximate area of 100 sq. miles. There was a native population, most of whom worked on the two copra plantations. Copra is the name given to the white of the coconut, which the natives removed and deposited in the drying sheds. The ample green vegetation made it an ideal place for castaways.

Meanwhile, on the "Orion" we heard the shattering news. A total of 514 prisoners had been released. It came as a great shock. I experienced an indescribable feeling of horror and frustration, realising we weren't going ashore with the rest. My first reaction was to think that Captain Weyher had denied our freedom in revenge for the fight back of the "Turakina". I believed he had included us in the category of the Armed Forces, rather than being civilian merchant seaman. I suppose he had a point, bearing in mind our 4.7" gun and our spirited response to his demand to surrender.

**ORION** DISGUISED WITH TWO FUNNELS

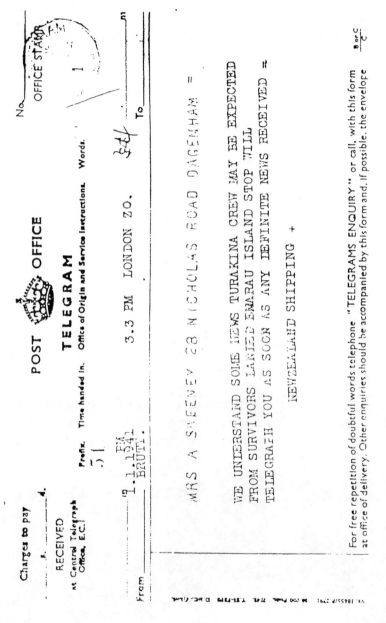

Charges to pay

£    s.    d.

RECEIVED
at Central Telegraph
Office, E.C.1

POST OFFICE

TELEGRAM

Prefix.    Time handed in.    Office of Origin and Service Instructions.    Words.

51    3.3 PM LONDON 20.

PM
12.1.1941
BRUTI.

From _____    To _____

No. _____

OFFICE STAMP

MRS A SWEENEY 28 NICHOLAS ROAD DAGENHAM =

WE UNDERSTAND SOME NEWS TURAKINA CREW MAY BE EXPECTED
FROM SURVIVORS LANDED EMIRAU ISLAND STOP WILL
TELEGRAPH YOU AS SOON AS ANY DEFINITE NEWS RECEIVED =

NEWZEALAND SHIPPING +

For free repetition of doubtful words telephone "TELEGRAMS ENQUIRY" or call, with this form
at office of delivery. Other enquiries should be accompanied by this form and, if possible, the envelope

B or C
C

102

We were also told he had rigidly opposed the release of any prisoners, without exception. He reasoned that vital information concerning the raiders' whereabouts and movements would be made known to the Allies. He argued that this would make their own position even more hazardous and insecure. His reasoning later proved correct.

Captain Eyssen of the "Komet" was his superior officer, so there was probably a compromise. Most of the prisoners on the "Orion" would stay, except for the coloured men. The majority of those on the "Kulmerland" and the "Komet" would be put ashore. This arrangement excluded any military personal, who were transferred to the "Orion". I still held out hope that our continued detention was only temporary and our release would follow later. The outlook was not too bright.

After going ashore at 3.pm, the majority had an eight mile walk to the opposite side of the island. The remainder, including women, children and some casualties, were transported by truck. Living in that area, were two white families, the Cooks and the Colletts. The men were managers at the two plantations. One was owned by the Australian Government, while the other belonged to a private Company. The number of native inhabitants would have been around five hundred. Most came from New Guinea, where even as late as the 1920's, head hunters and cannibals lived amongst them.

There was ample fish in the lagoons and with wild boar, fresh tropical fruit, including melons and pineapples, there was an abundance of good food available. The island had no radio equipment and therefore had no news or means of immediate communication with the outside world. This fact suited the Germans admirably. Before leaving this paradise, the Germans left behind a lifeboat, with a stark warning not to contact the Australian or New Zealand authorities for at least twenty-four hours.

Ignoring this instruction would have meant their prompt return and a heavy bombardment. Their homes and possessions would be completely destroyed. The inhabitants, unbeknown to the Germans, possessed a large diesel launch. Upon seeing the approach of the strange vessels and the invaders, it was covered over, completely hidden from prying eyes.

The following day, after completion of the twenty-four hour delay, the launch was dispatched to Kavieng, a port of New Ireland, some seventy miles away. This island was also a part of the Bismarck Archipelago. At Kavieng radio station, the respective authorities of Australia and New Zealand were immediately notified of the turn of events.

Subsequently, on Christmas Eve, the ketch "Leander" arrived from New Ireland fully loaded with stores and equipment. It included medical supplies and food and cigarettes which were in very short supply. A doctor was landed to supervise and assist in the welfare and care of the sick and injured. Christmas Day was spent in festive spirit, with the survivors thankful to be free. A few days later, all the ex prisoners embarked on the S. S. "Nellore" 8,000 tons, owned by the Eastern and Australian Line. She regularly sailed the busy route between Australia and Singapore.

After a short stay in Rabaul, New Britain, on New Year's Day, they arrived at Townsville, in Queensland Australia. It was a hot summer's day, as they received a tumultuous welcome from the cheering crowds thronging the shores. As well as large numbers of excited people, hundreds of boats of all shapes and sizes, decked with colourful flags and bunting came to greet them.

The joyful shouts of the onlookers were accompanied by the sounds of ships' sirens and horns coming from all directions. A wonderful sight to witness and hear. For those fortunate to be back home with their loved ones, their ordeal was over. For me, it was just the beginning.

# A MEETING AT A PACIFIC ATOLL

On the 23rd December, the "Orion" had left the tropical island of Emirau, for an arranged meeting at the Lamotrek atoll. That night, the seas were smooth, and we were all very quiet, thinking what might have been. I had mixed feelings. Downhearted and disillusioned, I thought of the fortunate people who'd earlier been freed. At the same time, I was pleased for them, particularly for the women and children, soon to be home with their families.

Lying in my hammock in the darkness, a voice suggested that we cheer ourselves by each singing a popular song of the day. After a while, everyone joined in with gusto, if not very tunefully. Possessing a deep voice, I remember giving my impression of Bing Crosby singing, "When the deep purple falls!" I was pleased though, when everyone joined in. The singing seemed to ease my disappointment and I fell into a deep sleep. Christmas Day came and went. Even our poor monotonous diet remained the same. As far as our captors were concerned, for us it was just another day. It was no different from the rest. Definitely, not a happy Christmas.

On leaving Emirau, the three ships parted company. The "Komet", on the 27th December, heavily shelled Nauru almost destroying the phosphate plant. Gigantic fires started and considerable damage was caused to many parts of the undefended island. Oil tanks were set alight, with the loss of 15,000 tons of oil. Essential phosphate supplies were halted for many weeks. The phosphates of Nauru are a salt of phosphoric acid, used mainly in artificial fertilisers. Months later in 1942, Nauru was invaded and occupied by the Japanese.

Having exhausted her supplies, the "Kulmerland" left Emirau and set a course for Japan, reaching her destination safely on the 31st December. On the same date, eight days after leaving Emirau, we arrived at the Lamotrek atoll. For the second time, there were three German ships at a rendezvous. Accompanying the "Orion", was the new supply ship, "Regensburg" and the large tanker, "Ole Jacob", 8,000 tons. It was New Years Eve, but again there were no celebrations for us. Nobody bothered to stay awake to see in the New Year. Unlike conditions on the "Komet" and "Kulmerland", there was no radio available for us to hear the celebrations. The only news we received was verbal propaganda from our captors.

Over the next few days, we were kept well below decks, where conditions were unbearable. We suffered extreme heat and discomfort, while oil was pumped aboard from the "Ole Jacob". The German crew worked under the hot tropical sun, unloading various commodities from the "Regensburg". On the 5th January, we were unaware of a new arrival and its significance. A fourth German ship had arrived at the atoll.

On the following afternoon, I was amazed when told to collect all personal belongings. I thought we were being set free. On being escorted on deck, I didn't expect to see the other German vessels. I wondered what had happened to our naval forces. It was very calm and humid, with a slight warm breeze. I was disappointed seeing just blue seas surrounding us. No beautiful islands with gentle swaying palm trees in sight.

Instead, along with another 182 prisoners, grim faced guards rushed us aboard the latest arrival, watched curiously and intently by other German crew members. Once again we were locked below. The future was not looking too bright. The 4½ stressful months on the "Orion" was not a very pleasant experience, to say the least. The food had been poor and there were times when the Germans were themselves short of essential supplies, including precious drinking water.

This shortage was directly caused by the large quantities required to satisfy the demands of the numbers of prisoners taken. It was the obvious solution to disembark the majority on Emirau. Apart from the survivors in our quarters, we were denied contact with other detainees. I had no personal belongings, just the clothes I wore when the "Turakina" was attacked. In the colder spells, I came to appreciate my warm seamen's jersey, with the initial NZSC displayed in red letters on my chest.

During the time spent on the "Orion", we had no reason to complain about the attitude of the German sailors. There was no ill treatment of any kind during our enforced stay. It would be fair to record their friendliness towards us, rather than them being known as the hated enemy. Their precarious position was the same as ours. Far from home, with an uncertain future. All of us being seamen, I think there was a common bond, combined with a mutual respect. On one occasion, upon complaining about the food, we were told that at that particular time, the crew were on the same rations as ourselves. At the time I doubted that was a true statement though.

After being escorted by German naval destroyers and submarines during the latter part of her journey, the "Orion" safely reached the port of Bordeaux in occupied France, on August 23rd 1941. She and her valiant crew had spent 510 eventful days at sea. During that time, they travelled 127,337 miles, sinking 73,500 tons of shipping, a total that included the joint sinking with the "Komet". Captain Weyher was personally awarded the Iron Cross medal by Adolph Hitler. He was later promoted, becoming the youngest ever Admiral of the German Navy. Other members of his crew were honoured and also awarded the Iron Cross for outstanding bravery. In 1942, the "Orion" became a "Werkstattschiff" (Workshop ship) and was renamed "Hektor". Two years later she changed to an artillery training school ship. On the 30th April 1945, she was bombed and sunk during an air raid off Swinemunde, Poland. In 1952, the "Hecktor", ex "Orion", was broken up and demolished by the Poles.

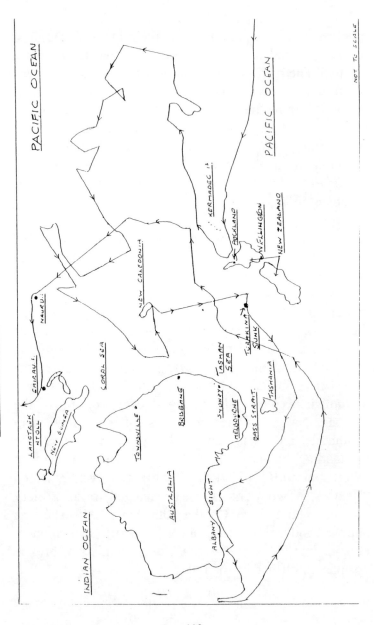

PART CRUISE OF GERMAN RAIDER ORION 1940

PACIFIC OCEAN

PACIFIC OCEAN

NOT TO SCALE

INDIAN OCEAN

LAMOTREK ATOLL

NEW GUINEA

RABAUL

NAURU

CORAL SEA

KERMADEC I.

AUCKLAND

WELLINGTON

NEW ZEALAND

NEW CALEDONIA

T.BAKINA SUNK

TASMAN SEA

AUSTRALIA

TOWNSVILLE

BRISBANE

SYDNEY

MELBOURNE

BASS STRAIT

TASMANIA

ALBANY BIGHT

110

**HEKTOR** EX-ORION, UNDER RAF ATTACK IN POLAND

# CHAPTER 6

## STORMY CAPE HORN

The newcomer was the passenger ship "Ermland", not to be confused with a second "Ermland". It is most unusual for ships of a country to have the same name. The latter was a large German Naval tanker, over 11,000 tons, capable of a top speed of 24 knots. She was one of four sister ships built and hurriedly completed in Danzig Poland in 1939. These large tankers were purpose built to supply submarines, surface raiders, pocket battleships and the heavy battle-cruisers. Their cargo would include food, clothing and other essential commodities. Huge tanks carried oil and fresh water, while mines, torpedoes, ammunition and spare parts were always readily available. If necessary, even a seaplane could be provided. Each ship was able to accommodate large numbers of Allied prisoners, enabling them to be transported to Occupied France. From there they would eventually be entrained to detention camps in Germany.

Our new prison was the much smaller vessel of 6,528 grt, owned by the Hamburg-Amerika Line. Built by Messrs Blohm and Voss at Hamburg in 1921, her German Commander was Captain Krage. The "Ermland" sailed from Kobe, Japan on 28th December 1940, after being adapted to accommodate 350 captives. I was unaware that with her consignment of prisoners, there would be an attempt to beat the blockade of Europe. On the 7th January 1941, the "Ermland" replenished the "Orion" with more supplies and the four ships then sailed together from the Lamotrek atoll. Two days later, we left the German convoy to continue our voyage alone. There was no information from the guards, so we could only conjecture as to the destination. There was still hope of the tropical island possibility, but it was appearing most unlikely.

The conditions were no better than the "Orion", but no worse. The only consolation was that, to my intense relief, there would be no more ear-splitting gun-fire to shatter the nerves. We were still confined and locked down below decks, except for the occasional hour on deck. Instead of a hammock, I slept on a hair mattress laid directly on the deck. Although uncomfortable, it was clean and appeared new. Each morning I would roll it up, stowing it against the ship's side. Having become accustomed to the hammock over the previous months, I preferred that arrangement, rather than the hard mattress.

Bare wooden tables and forms provided the only furniture, with showers and separate toilets close by. I was pleased to be issued with a new tooth brush, drinking glass, safety razor and a packet of blades. The razor blades were especially scarce. Speaking to a friendly guard, he demonstrated how to keep an edge on the blade. Placing it inside the glass, he pressed down hard, using his forefinger and pushed the blade firmly from side to side in short quick movements. As blades were like gold dust, it proved a useful tip.

In those days, everyone smoked cigarettes. At that time, no-one knew that smoking caused cancer. The brand of tobacco mostly purchased on the "Turakina" was called "Old Friend", packed in large upright tins. They were "roll your own", rather than the "tailor made" cigarettes I was used to. Occasionally, an amiable guard would offer someone a decent cigarette. It would be handed round six or seven men, each taking a long drawn out puff, before it was passed to the next person. The red hot ash never had time to cool.

On one occasion, longing for a cigarette, I took some horse hair from the mattress and wrapped it in toilet paper. My experiment was not repeated a second time!.

The Norwegian supply of American cigarettes had long been exhausted. Our craving was partly satisfied with the issue of the one packet a week of the strong Russian brand, still guaranteed to bring on an instant bout of coughing. During the long months spent playing cards, I probably learned every game that existed. Most popular were Rummy, Bridge, Whist, Nap, Eucre, Hearts, Five Hundred and Patience. Living under such conditions, patience was also a quality often sorely tried, particularly whenever a difference of opinion occurred.

Most days, when the weather was favourable, and circumstances permitted, we were allowed on deck for a short period for much needed fresh air. It was always a relief, escaping the humidity and boredom in our confined quarters. On these occasions, guards with machine guns were always in attendance, keeping a watchful eye on our movements. We were confined to the well deck, which allowed the guards to overlook the scene from the upper decks. The menacing guns were held ready, to combat any signs of revolt.

We were visited by a smartly uniformed person, who introduced himself as the Prison Officer. He was young, fair haired, with rather an arrogant attitude. He wasn't too friendly either, and was classed as a typical Nazi, nothing like the majority we had experienced to date. On his orders, each morning at 10am, we had to assemble in our quarters, standing to attention in four lines, to form a square. Accompanied by a guard, he would descend the ladder, saying "Good morning all." We replied with a loud chorus of "Guten Morgen", as he slowly began his inspection. To his credit though, it was never "Heil Hitler". On one occasion, while he was carrying out his duties, someone unfortunately couldn't restrain himself. The silence was broken by a very loud raspberry. It was difficult to contain our laughter. He wasn't amused though. As a punishment, we were barred from going on deck for four days and put on bread and water only over the same period. After that incident, there were no further problems.

Every Sunday, there would be a regular Church service with prayers and hymns. It was conducted by Padre E. R. Ball, who had been a passenger on the "Rangitane". He had not been put ashore on Emirau with the other survivors, as Captain Weyher considered him a member of the Armed Forces. The most popular hymn sung on each occasion was "Oh hear us when we cry to thee, for those in peril on the sea". I doubt whether a hymn has been sung with so much fervour and feeling as we expressed on those Sunday mornings. I used to look forward to the Padre's visits. I found solace and comfort in his words, giving us hope by putting our trust in the Lord. Catholic or Protestant, it made no difference, we were united in our prayers. Before the end of the war, Padre Ball was repatriated in a mutual exchange with other German prisoners held by the Allies.

After sailing steadily for two weeks, the weather had become much cooler, with the temperature dropping considerably. It made our living conditions much more bearable after suffering so many weeks in the stifling tropical heat. Just like the "Orion", the portholes were covered and screwed tightly shut. No views to be seen of the outside world from that source. Neither was there entertainment of any sort. No relayed music, radio, news bulletins, not even information on how the war was progressing. The Germans never enlightened us on that score, whether it be good news or bad, depending on whose side you were on.

Having worked at Sainsbury, it was my job to cut the large German sausage into equal amounts per person. Needless to say, I had to ensure my portion was no larger than others. Sometimes tempers would fray, and a heated argument would occur, mostly over some trivial item mentioned during a normal conversation. It never led to anything serious and allowed those involved to let off steam, probably for the best. The hour on deck when permitted, was our only escape from the trauma of being locked in our quarters. With little else to occupy our minds, the uncertainty of our future aggravated these situations.

The time came to wear my heavy jersey again, with the weather changing for the worse. It became extremely cold, and unfortunately, there was little heating. At night I would sleep fully clothed in a vain attempt to keep warm. Once again we experienced very bad storms, with the "Ermland" tossed about alarmingly as she battled through the gigantic waves. A few days passed, then a young friendly guard mentioned we had rounded Cape Horn and had later sailed quite close to the Falkland Islands. From that information we deduced that we were sailing in a northward direction, but we were still unaware of our final destination. Thankfully, the violent windy weather gradually abated and we moved serenely on an even keel.

As each day passed, with the daily rise in temperature, the hot sweaty conditions returned. It was always a relief when allowed on deck, whatever the weather. When under way, there was usually a nice breeze, albeit sometimes a hot one. On the 1st March, it came as a complete surprise when the vessel suddenly cut engines, then drifted for a short time before eventually coming to a dead stop. All was very quiet and still and an optimistic thought went through my mind. "Maybe it's my turn to be freed". South America would suit me fine!

# AN ANXIOUS WAIT IN THE ATLANTIC

Over the next seven days, we lay perfectly still, rolling silently and gently in the calm seas. What was going on? Once again we suffered from oppressive heat. I came to the conclusion the freezing cold was more to my liking. We had hove to in the middle of the South Atlantic ocean, our position being 26'30'S. 13010'E, some 650 miles north of Tristan da Cuna.

At this previously arranged meeting was the large German supply ship, the tanker "Nordmark", a sister ship to the Kriegsmarine "Ermland". The "Nordmark" was disguised as an American tanker, painted all over grey, the standard colour of United States tankers. On her sides, in large letters, was her adopted name, "Dixie". The "Nordmark" regularly took on this particular disguise but, on occasions would change the name to "Prairie".

It has been alleged and actually published that four United States tankers had waited in the Atlantic to supply the German war-ship "Bismarck", prior to her final voyage. It was also alleged the "Prairie" had refuelled a group of U-boats, including the U.107, six months before the U.S.A entered the war. However, both statements were incorrect. It was actually the German "Nordmark", operating under her disguise. On 8th March, we were joined at our anchorage by the warship "Admiral Scheer". A large number of prisoners were quickly transferred from her to the "Nordmark", en route for France.

Since October 27$^{th}$ 1940, the "Admiral Scheer" had sailed 46,419 miles, sinking 17 ships. On April 1$^{st}$ 1941, she reached Kiel in Germany , successfully evading detection by the allies. After an extensive refit, the battleship later patrolled the Baltic, assisting the German Army with heavy bombardment of Russian troops and shore defences. In April 1945 she met her end. Attacked by the Royal Air Force at Kiel in Germany, she caught fire, sinking in shallow water, and was completely destroyed. Later, the once regal battleship was broken up and sold for scrap.

In the meantime, in a combined effort to beat the blockade to Europe, the German tankers "Ermland" and "Altmark" were escorted on the latter part of their journey by two huge battle cruisers, the "Scharnhorst" and "Gneisnau". The warships then parted company from the tankers and proceeded to Brest, France, where they arrived on 22nd March 1941. The two tankers then made their way to La Rochelle on the west coast of France, where they also berthed unchallenged the following day, with all their prisoners safe and unharmed.

GERMAN BATTLESHIP **ADMIRAL SCHEER**

Meanwhile, once the transfer of prisoners was completed in the Atlantic, it was also time for us to continue our journey northwards. As time passed, we realised the tropical island was just a dream. There was only one frightening conclusion: we were on our way to Germany. This was later confirmed by a boastful guard declaring a phrase well known to many Allied prisoners, "For you the war is over."

Rumours began to circulate. Through the grapevine, we had information that our destination was Bordeaux, in Occupied France. As the days went by, there was a common feeling doubting whether the Germans would make it. We were aware of the might of our navy, with ample submarines and surface warships. The thought of an attack by the R.A.F was also a daunting prospect. As far as we knew, our "Ermland" had no means of defence. Some even thought we might be rescued before reaching port, but although our hopes were dashed, thankfully our worst fears were not fulfilled either.

On the forenoon of April 3rd, almost a month after parting from the "Admiral Scheer", we sailed quietly up the Gironde, reaching the comparative safety of Bordeaux. We were barred from going on deck and stayed on board overnight. I found it impossible to sleep, thinking only of the traumatic events of the past. After nearly eight months continuously at sea, I missed the noise of the propellers and the constant rolling aboard ship.

I found it hard to believe our good fortune, having survived all those hazards and dangers, but I couldn't understand how we'd travelled those thousands of miles across the oceans, without ever being challenged. I remembered the German crew on the "Orion", thinking that I would not wish to be in their shoes. However, like us, they were just performing their duty. Next morning, I would at last step on dry land, albeit still a prisoner of war, unsure of what the future might hold.

As for the ex passenger motor vessel "Ermland", in 1942 she was commandeered by the German Navy (Kriegsmarine). Used extensively as a supply ship, she sailed under the new name of "Weserland". In 1944, off Ascension Island in the South Pacific, she sank after being scuttled by her own crew.

# CHAPTER 7

## PRISON CAMP STALAG 221

At last the morning came.  It was time to go ashore.  A fantastic moment, as with mixed feelings of elation and relief, I walked slowly down the steep, rickety gangway. For some seconds, walking on solid ground was a peculiar sensation, and I felt rather giddy.  After nearly eight months of constantly swaying in harmony with the pitching and rolling of the German ships at sea, it seemed my body was not prepared for the lack of movement underfoot.  However, the feeling soon passed.  It was wonderful to see a few other vessels tied up in the docks. Everything seemed so quiet and normal.  It was a sight I never thought to see again.

My elation abruptly came to an end when I saw,  waiting on the quayside, stood a number of grim faced, jack-booted German soldiers, dressed in their sombre grey uniforms.  All were well armed, prominently displaying their guns.  The Army had now taken over from the Navy and I felt it could be for the worse.  The thought of being a prisoner of war for the duration, was a prospect I was not looking forward to. Who could tell how long the war would last? Something inside me suggested it could be a long conflict. The future appeared decidedly bleak, and the first thoughts of an escape went through my mind.

Lined up alongside some huge deserted sheds were a number of buses. We were searched, counted, then hurriedly escorted on board. At this stage, I thought we might be driven all the way to Germany. Never told of their plans for us, it was always a question of, "Wait and see!" Accompanied by two burly guards, one sitting sideways in front with the driver and the other standing at the rear, we sped through the deserted villages on the outskirts of Bordeaux. Travelling along tree lined roads, I marvelled at the sight. I had not seen a tree since leaving Australia.

I thought how attractive the buildings and houses looked. There was little road traffic, with most people riding bicycles. Some pedestrians, although looking rather subdued, were engaged in their everyday affairs. It was a wonderful sight to behold. In the real world, in normal circumstances, all these insignificant things are taken for granted. How I longed to be free again, back home in England. Passing through the town of Bordeaux, we headed along the main road. After travelling a few miles, the bus slowed as it approached two large areas, enclosed by tall, barbed wire fences. We had finally reached our destination. A German transit camp.

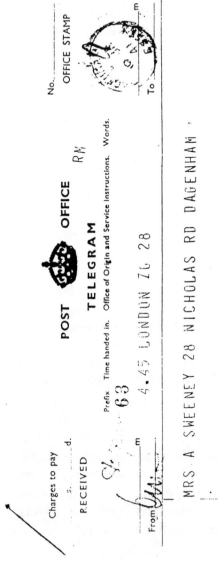

POST OFFICE

**TELEGRAM**

Charges to pay
£. . . d.

RECEIVED

From

Prefix   Time handed in.   Office of Origin and Service Instructions.   Words.

63        4.45  LONDON  26  28

No.

OFFICE STAMP

To

RM

MRS A SWEENEY 28 NICHOLAS RD DAGENHAM ·

= MR E J SWEENEY REPORTED BY MINISTRY OF SHIPPING
THROUGH INTERNATIONAL RED CROSS SAFE BUT PRISONER OF
WAR = NEWZEALAND SHIPPING COMPANY +

28 +

) of doubtful words telephone " TELEGRAMS ENQUIRY " or call, with this form     B or C
at office of delivery. Other enquiries should be accompanied by this form and, if possible, the envelope.     C

126

It was here large numbers of captured Allied prisoners were brought to be later accommodated in a more permanent site in Germany. The camp consisted of two compounds each situated either side of the main thoroughfare to Bordeaux. Situated amongst the abundant, magnificent pine trees, it was a very beautiful setting. Unfortunately, the conditions inside the camp were a stark contrast.

Each compound was surrounded by two fences of heavy gauge barbed wire. A gap of about four feet between the fences was filled with large coils of the same deadly wire. It would have been impossible to overcome that particular hazard. High wooden platforms were erected at each corner, which provided the guards with a commanding view of the whole area. They possessed machine guns and searchlights, while more steel helmeted soldiers patrolled the perimeter. Taking in the scene, it reminded me of American prison films I had seen before the war.

With shouts to get a move on, we were quickly marched through the large metal gates into the compound. Guards hustled and shepherded us into forming a long orderly queue in the open grounds. There was another head count and a further search for hidden weapons. Once at the head of the queue, I faced two young German Officers. They were smartly dressed in their smooth serge uniforms, wearing caps with bright red bands and highly exaggerated peaks. Their jackboots were well polished and, sitting calmly and sternly at a large trestle table, they appeared very business like and efficient. A number of armed soldiers were in attendance, keeping a watchful eye on the proceedings.

The expected interrogation proved to be just an identification parade, as one Officer noted my name, age, place of birth and my ship. Moving along in the queue, the second Officer politely inquired, " Do you possess anything of value? If so", he explained, "It will be confiscated for safe keeping and you will be given a receipt. Valuable possessions will be returned once the war is over."

I thought at the time that it was a rather dubious statement, hard to believe. I doubted their integrity. In fact, in most cases, at the end of hostilities possessions actually were returned to their rightful owners. On learning I had no papers, money or valuables, I was abruptly dismissed by a guard. In a loud hoarse voice, he impatiently barked, "Hurry along please". After the interview, we were marched to our huts and finally left to our own devices.

The accommodation consisted of six large shed-like blocks built in the centre of each compound. They were originally constructed by the French gun powder factory who had requisitioned many areas in St. Medard, with the permission of the local council. The factory had also built many similar huts at the time of the first World War, but most had been disposed of after the Armistice was signed in 1918.

THE NEW ZEALAND SHIPPING Co.Ld.
(INCORPORATED IN NEW ZEALAND.)

TELEGRAPHIC ADDRESS,
"DELECTABLE, STOCK, LONDON."

TELEPHONE No. 8880 AVENUE.

ALL COMMUNICATIONS TO BE ADDRESSED
The General Managers

138, Leadenhall Street.
London, E.C.3.

18th September, 1940.

Mrs. J Quinn,
   89, Kenilworth Road,
     Lanark.

Dear Sir or Madam,

     We have been informed by the Admiralty
that they have no further news of the s.s. "TURAKINA"
and we are asked by them to notify you that the
ship must therefore, be presumed to have been lost
by enemy action.

     The Admiralty however state that there
is every reason to believe that most of the crew
are prisoners of war.

     The moment any information reaches us we
will at once inform you.

       Yours faithfully,

       T.F. Tallents.
     for the General Managers.

129

THE NEW ZEALAND SHIPPING C? L?
(INCORPORATED IN NEW ZEALAND.)

*Telegrams & Cables. Doubtable. Stock. London.*
*Telephone No. 5220 Avenue*

ALL COMMUNICATIONS TO BE ADDRESSED
THE GENERAL MANAGERS

138, Leadenhall Street,
London, E.C.3.

12th June, 1941

Mrs. A. Sweeney,
  28, Nicholas Road,
      Dagenham

Dear Mrs. Sweeney,

Now that Mr. E.J. Sweeney is known to be a prisoner in Germany, you will naturally wish to know what arrangements we propose to make about his pay.

The Government are at present placing to "reserve" for him the sum of £1. per month so that there may be something for him to draw when he comes home. They will also arrange for him to draw £1. per month in Reichmarks whilst he is in camp in Germany.

The New Zealand Shipping Company will also credit him with the same amount, i.e. £1. per month, and invest it in War Savings Certificates or in an account with the Post Office Savings Bank.

It is not yet certain how many months full pay will be credited to him by the Government but the scheme set out above will operate as soon as his pay from the Government ceases.

In present conditions we cannot pledge the Company indefinitely; but this scheme will continue at any rate until February next and thereafter we shall do all we can to continue it.

It would not doubt be a relief to his mind if you could convey to him that you are satisfied with the arrangements that have been made.

You will have heard from the Red Cross that parcels of clothing and food are sent by them to prisoners-of-war camps. The next-of-kin of each prisoner has, however, the privilege of sending once a quarter through the Red Cross a personal parcel up to 10 lbs. in weight including the packing. The notice you should have had from the Red Cross tells you what may be put in the parcel and how it should be packed and sent off. Do not put in the parcel anything not allowed by the instructions as, if you do so, the parcel cannot be sent off. You will probably wish to make up this parcel yourself but if you prefer it you may send any articles you want to put in it (provided they are allowed by the regulations) together with the labels and that you will receive from the Red Cross to Messrs. Duncan Wallet & Co. 18, South Tenter Street, E.1. who will repack it and send it off to the Red Cross, completing it to full weight at the expense of the New Zealand Shipping Company if you are unable to manage that yourself.

Books, smokes and games can be sent direct from certain approved dealers under other schemes, particulars of which can be obtained from the Red Cross. We propose to supplement any of these supplies that you may wish to send yourself by arranging to send once a quarter a parcel of books and a parcel of games and once a fortnight 4 oz. of tobacco or cigarettes. It would be a help if you would let Messrs. Duncan Wallet & Co. know whether Mr. Sweeney is likely to prefer

130

At the beginning of the Second World War, the gun powder factory applied to requisition more land to build additional premises. A farmer living in St. Medard had then written to the council strongly objecting to the proposal. He pointed out that he was a stock breeder and milk producer, and would have no room for his 26 cows. Having hired the ground for twelve years, grazing his cattle, the thought of his meadows being taken over caused him a great deal of concern, but it was to no avail.

After the French surrender, the German army took over the majority of these huts and the accompanying land. It was a simple matter to adapt them for their own particular purpose, either as ready made prison camps or military barracks.

As I entered my hut it felt cold and damp, with a musty smell prevailing. Bare boards were fixed at right angles to each long wall, leaving a narrow passage-way about one metre wide, running through the centre. Scruffy, dirty canvas mattresses, filled with straw, completely flattened out of shape, were laid directly and uninvitingly on the bare boards.

The number of so called beds was doubled up by an extra tier built above the lower bunks. There were no chairs and no table, the only concession, one tattered smelly blanket per person. A large tin plate had been placed on each person's bunk. The small windows allowed some daylight to enter but, with the completely bare walls and the dim light that existed day and night, it was cheerless and dismal.  It was hardly conducive to promoting a settled or optimistic frame of mind.

Although it was extremely cold at night, no form of heating was available.  At the far end of the hut, there was a rusty, broken stove, with a narrow chimney stack protruding and disappearing through the ceiling.  Being so miserably cold, particularly during the long dark hours, it would have provided a welcome source of warmth.  In an area close to the outside of the camp, the Germans had felled a number of pine trees, creating a large clearing.  Logs were stacked neatly in huge piles, but our request for any form of fuel was ignored by the strict camp Commander.  A few logs would have spared us some misery.

At one end of the hut just inside the entrance, stretching almost the whole width, stood our washing facility.  It consisted of a low tank about four metres in length, with one tap and a shower.  They provided just a dribble of cold water.  It was impossible to shower as the trickle of water was so inadequate.  Hot water was unavailable.  I dreamed of a nice hot bath, working up the foamy bubbly water with a huge bar of soap.  In fact, soap was like gold-dust, with a ration of one tablet each day.  Shared amongst 100 men, the bar disappeared in a short space of time.

Clothes were washed in the basin, using cold water and without soap.  After eight months of continual wear and washing, my belongings were showing some signs of deterioration. I still possessed only the clothes I was wearing when the "Turakina" went down. They consisted of a white vest, a blue shirt that I seldom wore, (keeping it for special occasions!), one pair of dungarees, (a type of jeans), socks, shoes and my trusty jersey. I do not know how I would have survived without it. I could however, have made use of a needle and thread to darn my socks.

The German Officer in charge of the running of the camp, no doubt on the orders of his Government, classed us as civilians. Even on a German postcard, we were told to write our status as being civil internees. If we were not members of the armed forces, they were not compelled to give us the respect, treatment or privileges normally provided for army or naval personal.

Neither the British Government, the Red Cross, nor any other organisation were given any personal information regarding our internment in St. Medard en Jalles. On the 10th April, I was handed one German Kriegsgefangenen post-carte to send to my family, informing of my safety. I doubted whether it would be posted once the cards were collected. I was surprised and pleased to learn months later, that it arrived safely after a lapse of seven days. I still have the card in my possession, dated 11th April 1941.

The Red Cross were barred from entering the camp, but were allowed to hand in parcels for distribution amongst the prisoners, after the Germans had first helped themselves to what took their fancy.

Rumours suggested we wouldn't be in the transit camp for long before being transported to Germany. While in St. Medard, no official notification would be made of our whereabouts until we reached a permanent prison camp in Germany. Under the circumstances, we could hardly expect much assistance from any outside source. The rumours suggested we would probably be leaving within two weeks.

Thoughts of escape occasionally crossed my mind, but weighing up the situation, I accepted it was hardly an opportune time. Security was so tight, there was little chance of success. With guards continually patrolling the perimeter and, under the ever watchful eyes of the platform guards, an attempt to make a dash for it would have been suicidal. Digging a tunnel was not my idea of an easy means of escape, particularly without the tools to carry out such an operation. I did not think it was a practical solution. My main concern was the distance involved in tunnelling to a safe position outside the camp boundary. It would have been a long, arduous task to perform in the few days available.

Time was the most important factor. I guessed that when there were sufficient numbers of Allied prisoners to warrant a full train load, I would be on my way to a prison camp in Germany, undoubtedly for the duration of the war. In fact on the 3rd April, the same day that I arrived in Bordeaux, more than a thousand prisoners from the St. Medard camp were crowded on to one train, bound for Germany.

Some journeys, with prisoners herded into cattle trucks, would take four or five days before arriving at their destination. One point of arrival was at Bremervorde, from there, prisoners were marched about 14 kilometres to an established camp at Sandbostel. However, the thought of possibly many years in a prison camp in Germany, was not to my liking. I finally came to a decision. My mind was made up. I would attempt to escape if and when the opportunity arose.

In the meantime, back at the hut, Frank Quinn had grabbed the bunk next to mine. Frank was a dour, 20 year old ordinary seaman hailing from Lanark, Scotland. Being the same age, we had much in common and became good friends. Sitting on our hard wooden bunks, he said ruefully, "I don't about you Oz, but I'm starving". Although I had left Australia and emigrated to England some six years previously, I still spoke with a decided accent. As is usually the case, I was always known as "Oz" or "Aussie".

We decided to have a stroll around the site to get our bearings, and take a little exercise before lunch. Slowly making our way towards the perimeter, we came to a small wooden hut. The smell was unbearable. On opening the door, we realised it concealed the toilet, a large very deep hole dug in the ground. Inside, stretching across from one side to the other, was a thick, round wooden pole, on which one would precariously squat. A similar pole, much narrower, acted as a back rest. If you lost your balance, hard luck. It had been known to happen.

When the hole was almost full, the hut was lifted off, earth shovelled in and levelled. Another large hole was dug alongside, the wooden structure lifted bodily and repositioned. The obnoxious stench must have been noticed by people passing by. If the French had complained, I doubt whether it would have changed the situation.

While using the toilet, I would hold my hand tightly over my nostrils and mouth. It was a futile attempt to avoid breathing in the germs, but it helped to reduce the appalling odour. When a new pit was dug, the problem was not quite so bad.

On occasions there were long queues, particularly when we suffered from diarrhoea and sickness. There were also cases of dysentery.

Quickly leaving the area, we made our way back to our hut to await our meal. After a while the door opened slightly. A burly guard poked his head round, shouting for two men to collect our midday meal from the cookhouse. The two volunteers were marched off, while the remainder needed very little encouragement to assemble in file outside.

With watchful guards in attendance, I stood with stomach rumbling in the line close to the hut. Eagerly clutching the tin plate, I hoped for a substantial meal to satisfy my hunger. The kitchen was based in the next compound so, while we waited patiently, the two volunteer prisoners struggled back with a very large metal container. Two poles were fixed through the handles, making it easier to carry. Even so, it was extremely heavy and the men needed to stop every few paces for a rest.

On this occasion, it proved to be full of so called vegetable soup, but the vegetables were few and far between. In fact, it was boiled water, with an odd carrot or piece of turnip appearing on your plate, if it was your lucky day. There were times when you might receive the odd tiny portion of potato or maybe even a few potato peelings, and it would be like winning the lottery. The pan was turned upside down and scraped to extract every drop, then returned to the kitchen. Having finished the midday meal, I went back to the hut, rinsed my plate with cold water, shook it dry and laid it neatly at the head of my bunk in anticipation of the next meal.

Apart from the lack of food, I felt quite fit. Always an active but rather quiet, placid person, I possessed a very positive attitude and a strong will. It's been said that I am too independent, and I would not disagree with that assessment. I had learned to accept most things that happened in my life. Those attributes I believe stood me in good stead. I learned to calmly accept the problems as they arose and this principle and attitude of mind was a great help to me under the circumstances. I also found solace and comfort in my prayers.

At 4.30 that afternoon, two prisoners had been detailed to attend the kitchen. They were seen staggering towards our hut with a full container. There was a shout of "Tea up!", followed by a rush to form a queue outside. Dipping my plate into the container, I filled it to the brim, gulped it down, rejoining the queue along with the rest until the supply was exhausted. It was mint tea, hot and sweet, quite palatable, but did nothing to alleviate the pangs of hunger. There would be nothing else to eat or drink that day. The ever present guard, knowing how we felt, said sympathetically, "Maybe you will get bread tomorrow".

# R.A.F AIR RAIDS

There was nothing to do except to take another walk, this time keeping well away from the toilet area. With other detainees, we continually retraced our steps back and forth along the well worn track. It was quite pleasant just to watch people and traffic passing along the main road. So much so, although very hungry, I felt good to be alive. There was the occasional wave to any young females passing by. All would wave back, to the annoyance of the guards. Their response was always a loud angry shout in German, "It is forbidden!". However, it did not deter us or the girls. Probably the guards were just jealous.

Strict orders were given. Every prisoner had to occupy his hut by 8.30pm. It was very cold that evening, as I climbed into my bunk fully clothed, I had no pyjamas anyway, and I pulled the blanket around my shoulders trying to keep warm. It was still early April and, while laying shivering in my bed, I thought of the sweltering nights spent in the tropics, yearning for cooler conditions.

At 9pm, the German guard switched off the lights of our dimly lit quarters, and I tried to sleep. Some time later, I had almost dozed off when there was the sound of planes in the distance. I could tell they were bombers, by the drone of the engines. They were flying at a high altitude. Suddenly, there was an outbreak of fierce gunfire close by, as German anti-aircraft guns opened with a prolonged noisy barrage. I lay awake thinking how ironic it would be if, after all our trials and tribulations, we were to be bombed by our own people. However the aircraft soon passed over, the firing ceased, the searchlights faded, and the still and darkness of the night was restored.

The noisy air raids occurred most nights. The whole area would light up with the dropping of flares, accompanied by the criss-crossing searchlights as the Germans attempted to pinpoint their targets. It was impossible to learn if the sorties were successful, Jerry would not give us any information. We assumed the target was the Bordeaux area, possibly the docks. We just hoped that the raids were successful, and our planes and crews would return safely to the bases in England.

What with the explosive noise of the gunfire that first night, I couldn't sleep. The morning and daylight couldn't come soon enough. Maybe I could get some news of the intended transfer to Germany. I assumed that conditions there could not be worse than those at Stalag 221. The thoughts of an escape were now firmly entrenched in my mind, I would not fail to seize the opportunity if it arose. Eventually I fell into a deep sleep, to be awakened by the lights being switched on by a guard.

It was still dark outside, and I kept shivering in the freezing, dismal surroundings. Bleary eyed, tired, dishevelled and hungry, we patiently awaited our turn to wash or shower in the communal tub. Each person attempted to use as little of the meagre soap allowance as possible, to ensure there would be some left for those following on behind. To make matters worse, the trickle of bitterly cold water made it almost impossible to get a lather.

The darkness of the night receded and as the welcoming dawn approached our hopeless and desperate feelings abated despite the poor conditions in the camp

Our compound guard arrived and switched off the lights. About an hour later, he ordered us to assemble outside. It was time for roll call and inspection. A stern faced young Officer approached, accompanied by another guard. Firmly grasping some papers in one hand and a pen in the other, he ran his gaze disdainfully over each of us in turn. With some deliberation, he slowly counted our number ensuring there were no absentees. Having satisfied himself that the figures were correct, he made a few notes and then dismissed us with an arrogant wave of his hand. Abruptly clicking his feet together, he then made a smart about turn and marched off, with the guard meekly following three or four paces behind.

It was almost breakfast time, so we returned to the hut to collect our plates. Assembling outside again, we eagerly awaited the delivery of breakfast. It duly arrived, the same container filled this time with steaming hot ersatz coffee. It was rumoured to be made from acorns, but I'm not sure if that was true. It was quite drinkable though, the container was soon drained dry and returned. I turned to Frank and said jokingly, "I could eat a horse". He agreed, suggesting he would be glad of the opportunity. Apart from the tinned whale meat eaten on the German ships, I had been without fish, meat, whole vegetables, eggs and fruit for nearly 8 months.

The very welcome news suddenly emanating from the cookhouse, indicated there would be a bread issue, at about 10am that same morning. A momentous occasion. The ration for each person proved to be a chunk of dry black bread, about eight centimetres thick. It was the only solid food we'd get and was meant to last the whole day. Having eaten it on the German ships, I had become accustomed to the flavour and texture and had actually grown to enjoy it. However, it was not to everyone's liking. Even so, there was no doubt the bread would be an important and essential contribution to our daily diet.

The following day there was a visit by the Red Cross, but we were not allowed contact, but packages were handed to the guards at the gate. Some clothes and food parcels were left for the benefit of the prisoners. These were opened and distributed by the Germans, after they had selected certain items for themselves. Some biscuits and a small portion of cheese were most acceptable. I was also able to obtain an oversized, crumpled jacket, another shirt, socks and a pair of baggy fawn trousers. It was good to have the extra pair to change into, although I would have preferred another blanket, to provide extra warmth at night.

We kept ourselves quite fit taking long walks, as the monotonous and depressing days dragged by. Each one was a carbon copy of the previous, without exception. A couple of times though, for a change, we had turnip water soup. Very often, there was the hurried trip to the toilet only to find a long queue. If possible, for obvious reasons, it was advisable not to linger more than was necessary.

During our extensive walks, we must have covered many miles, stepping it out quite smartly along the well trudged paths. It probably stood us in good stead for our forthcoming escapades and adventures. Always in sight were the jack booted, steel helmeted guards, with rifles slung over their right shoulders, ever watchful for any sign of trouble.

They seemed an unsociable bunch and I felt they would need very little provocation before resorting to the use of their weapons. Maybe I misjudged them, for undoubtedly, being dedicated and well trained soldiers, they were under strict orders, just carrying out their normal allotted duties. I tried tackling our compound guard for any information concerning our future movements, but there was no news from that source. His uncompromising reply was always, "Later you will know". His words were prophetic. I had been living under the squalid and filthy conditions in the camp for eleven miserable days. It was a cold wintry morning when we assembled as usual for roll call. After satisfying himself there were no absentees, the Officer, without warning, said suddenly, "You are leaving, collect your belongings".

The curt statement was followed by the news we were being transferred to Germany. His words did come as a shock though, as the timing was so unexpected. It would not take up too much of my time getting packed, my possessions were practically nil. During the boring and degrading few days spent in the transit camp, there had been the opportunity of paying some German guards for greatly over-priced cigarettes, sweets and other similar luxuries. However, not having the necessary finance, I could never take advantage of their offers.

We were allowed to drink our coffee and take our bread allowance. Some biscuits supplied by the Red Cross were shared out equally, but still thinking of my intention to escape, I decided to keep mine for the train journey. The guard later entered, giving instructions to tidy up the hut. The blanket had to be folded neatly, with the tin plate resting on top. Both had to be placed at the head of the bed, ready for inspection. The object, evidently, was to make everything shipshape and ready to accommodate the next unfortunate batch of prisoners.

Later in the day came the order to assemble outside the hut for the last time. There was another roll call, and a quick body search. The immaculate fussy Officer had to satisfy himself there were no stragglers or potential escapees hiding in the hut. Convinced everything was to his liking, he eventually gave the order to march, and we were on our way. I took a last look round. To say I was not sorry to leave, would be an understatement. However, there was worse to come.

Telephone: Thornton 3241.

M.P.B.465.

Telegraphic Address:
"Warpension, Blackpool."

MINISTRY OF PENSIONS,
Norcross,
Blackpool, Lancs.

Reference 35/PN4/10263

19 MAY 1941    1941.

Madam,

    I am directed by the Minister of Pensions to inform you that in view of the 'detention' of your *son* consequent on the sinking of the s/s "*Zurichia*", his position has been considered under Part II of the War Pensions and Detention Allowances (Mercantile Marine, etc.) Scheme. Payment will be made to you provisionally, under this scheme of 9/2 *per week (Nine Shillings and twopence).* The allowance will be effective from *8/4/41* but will be subject to adjustment in respect of any payments under the Prevention and Relief of Distress Scheme, or other public monies which you may have received since that date.

Payment

Mrs A. Sweeney
28, Gibbeton Road,
Dagenham, Essex.

146

# CHAPTER 8

## AUF WIEDERSEHEN. THE FIRST ESCAPE

Escorted by a number of heavily armed guards, we eventually reached the small deserted station in the pretty village of St. Medard-en Jalles. Awaiting our arrival was an ancient locomotive, noisily hissing and emitting puffs of dirty black smoke while getting up steam. Coupled behind were a large number of green coloured coaches, rather old and dilapidated. I thought a good coat of paint would have enhanced their appearance. With the idea of escape still fresh in my mind, I had a stroke of good fortune. I was almost at the back of the queue as we marched along the platform. Upon orders being barked to halt, I found myself directly opposite the only unlocked door of the very last carriage. As the Germans shouted and urged us to hurry, I quickly scrambled aboard, with Frank following closely behind. Coupled to our coach was a brown painted guard's van. I realised that the only potential problem was that there may be armed soldiers to guard us on while we were inside the carriage.

My first impression was of the rows of hard uncomfortable wooden seats.  There were no separate compartments, so we were in full view of our guards.  A narrow passage ran down the centre.  I grabbed a position by the aisle, with my back to the rear of the train.  As the coach filled and all were seated, two armed guards entered.  One was of medium build, fair complexioned, and seemed quite amiable.  Unfortunately, the other was just the opposite, bull necked, red faced and arrogant looking.   He proceeded to count our numbers in a disdainful and aggressive manner, showing us he was in charge.  He fitted everyone's idea of a typical Nazi.

After checking all windows were tightly closed, he growled in a loud authoritative voice, "Anyone opening the window and poking his head out, will get it blown off.  There will be no warning."  I have no doubt he meant this.  The two guards positioned themselves at the far end of the carriage, facing towards us and the guard's van at the rear.  All doors of the coach were securely locked.

Shortly afterwards, once everyone was settled on board, there was a loud toot from the driver and the train noisily began to edge away from the platform.  Chugging away, puffing out intermittent frequent clouds of steam mingled with sooty black smoke, the old engine laboriously puffed through the green countryside. In a short while, we reached the busy main railway station of Bordeaux.  It was a brief stop, for after about fifteen minutes of shunting and being coupled to another engine, we continued on our journey.   The train moved slowly, crossing noisily over numerous points as we encountered and negotiated the busy junctions.   Finally, after greatly increasing speed, we had left the town and outlying districts far behind.   An opportune time to make another roll call.

It was to become a regular occurrence. As previously, he waggled his forefinger, pointing directly to each prisoner in turn, counting loudly in his guttural German language. His unpleasant cynical expression would change, giving way to a satisfied smirk, as he assured himself there were no absentees.  The hours passed quickly as I gazed at the peaceful open country, continuously flashing by the windows, in a never-ending panorama.  I was unaware I would soon be a part of that scene.   Eventually, the evening shadows began to close in, as the colourful reds and yellows of the sunset faded from view.  It had been a very cold day, but it was fine and dry.

Suddenly, the noisy rhythmic beat from the railway track lessened, as the train reduced speed.  I assumed it was due to a red light signal, or perhaps a cautionary go slow warning.  I peered ahead through the closed windows, and noticed the train was negotiating a bend in the track. It stretched in a long gradual curve to our right.

A thought immediately sprang to my mind. I could not be seen from most of the front carriages.  It meant climbing through the window on my left.  I turned to Frank saying, "This would be a good chance to escape".  In the dim light, I heard someone say, "Why don't you go then?" On the spur of the moment, I retorted, "OK, I will, are you coming Frank?" I didn't need to ask twice, he quickly agreed to follow me. I glanced at the guards, both had their backs turned and were deep in conversation.

I rose warily from my seat, watching for any movement from them. Trying not to make a sound, and with my heart in my mouth, I stepped over outstretched legs. A thick leather strap held the window in its closed position. Still with one eye on the Germans, I gently lifted the broad fastener off its hook. It seemed to take forever, but I slowly eased down the heavy glass window. The opening was not very large, and the base of the window was quite high above floor level. It made climbing through very difficult.

After some hurried ungainly attempts, I managed to awkwardly manoeuvre both legs through the small gap. Taking another quick glance at the guards, without further hesitation, I jumped feet first, stumbling forward, then fell headlong to the ground. It seemed to take a long time to fall, but it was only seconds. Although I had planned to escape when the opportunity arose, when it did occur, it was completely spontaneous.

I found myself lying on top of a steep sloping embankment, covered in long spindly growth. I lay perfectly still for a few moments, getting my breath back. I had fully expected to hear rifle or pistol shots being fired from the rear van at least. However, my fears were unfounded. With my heart beating madly, I raised my head, and watched the twinkling red rear light fade in the distance. The train rounded the bend and disappeared into the dark shadows of the night.

I couldn't help thinking of that burly guard, I would love to have seen his face when he next counted his prisoners. I could imagine his angry ravings when he discovered two of his charges missing. After months of humiliation and frustration in German captivity, a wonderful moment had arrived, at last it was Auf Wiedersehen and we were free. How long for would be another question. I realised there was still a long road to travel.

# LOST IN THE FOREST

I picked myself up rather gingerly, but although somewhat shaken by the fall, I was unharmed, no apparent physical damage. Frank had jumped immediately after me, but was not quite so lucky. He finished up in a narrow ditch after falling awkwardly and tumbling to the bottom of the embankment. His shoes and socks suffered the most, becoming soaking wet, which caused him some pain later. Apart from that mishap, he was otherwise unhurt.

I ran towards him as we spotted two shadowy figures in the distance. In the gloom, we could not tell where they were heading, who they were, or what they were doing. Frank said, "Lets go Oz". Our good fortune again stood us in good stead. Stretching alongside the railway track, about 100 metres away, was a dense forest. Without further ado, we jumped over the ditch and made a dash for the welcome sanctuary of the trees. We thought it unlikely that a search was being made, but having got so far, we were taking no chances.

It was comforting to have the seclusion and shelter, combined with the comparative safety that the eerie forest provided. With the closeness of the overhanging trees, it was very dark with poor visibility. There was a feeling of clammy dampness in the air and I shivered with the coldness of our surroundings. The rustling of the trees and other weird noises of the lonely forest and its inhabitants were very disconcerting. We became quite scared. With my teeth chattering, I said to Frank, "I'll glad when it's daylight again, I don't fancy a second night in this gloomy forest".

It was impossible to rest or sleep under these conditions, so there was no alternative but to keep walking. Being cold, the exercise helped to keep the circulation going and getting deeper into the forest would be to our advantage. If there was a search party, which I thought unlikely, the possibility of detection would be greatly reduced. We hoped our sense of direction would allow us to walk in a continuous straight line.

I seemed to remember, I once read an article, stating in this kind of situation, a person could actually keep walking in circles. Our strategy was to put as much distance as possible between us and the point of escape. In the morning, we hoped to observe the sunrise. This would help us to get our bearings, enabling us to head in a southerly direction. Not knowing where the train was headed, we had no idea of our location. We concluded we were still in the northern part of Occupied France, possibly not far from the border. After walking for hours, there was still no sign of civilisation. We speculated about the size of the forest, maybe it stretched for 50 to 100 kilometres. Only time would tell.

Doubts were now entering our minds. Suppose we were walking around in circles and couldn't find a way out. Frank said with a grin, "I hope we're not lost". Shortly afterwards, he complained that his feet were very sore, and making walking difficult and painful due to marching most of the night in wet socks. We were compelled to move at a much slower pace, as he was limping quite badly. He never mentioned the problem again, but I could see he was struggling with the pain and discomfort. Under the circumstances, and in almost complete darkness, we walked closer together, side by side. We had no wish to become separated.

Feeling tired and dispirited, daylight and the accompanying warmth of the morning could not come soon enough. Shivering and trudging wearily on, some hours later we were gladdened by the sight of a few small shafts of light filtering through the trees. At last dawn was approaching and we were cheered at the sight. From the little we could see of the sky, it appeared cloudless. It seemed we could be in for a nice warm Spring morning.

We found a dry spot and sat down to take a well earned rest. Frank removed his socks, hanging them on a branch of a tree, to allow them to dry thoroughly. His feet were very red and sore, with the skin rubbed off in places. No wonder it was painful! As the sun rose, we peered through the dense foliage and were able to get a fairly good idea of the southerly direction we needed.

Our minds were more settled once we'd established our approximate route. The forest had to end somewhere and all the while that the sun was in our sight, we would keep on the right track. After about an hour, we felt more relaxed and refreshed. Frank carefully got to his feet, checked his socks, said they were completely dry and that he was ready to carry on.

After about an hours walk we suddenly came across a large open clearing. I thought it could be a picnic area, although there were no facilities to be seen. A few narrow paths branched off in different directions. Eagerly choosing one of the winding, well trodden tracks, I wondered where it would lead.

By this time, Frank's feet, although still sore, were much easier. We walked a little faster hoping we'd finally be clear of the forest. Carrying on for a few more minutes, with the trees gradually thinning out, I knew that we were nearing the edge of the woods. It was such a relief to know we weren't lost after all. As we rounded a bend in the track, directly ahead was the glorious sight of the open fields. My spirits rose as I took in the bright daylight. A sight for sore eyes. It was still very early morning, quiet, with the trees rustling and swaying gently in a slight breeze. There were no signs of people or traffic. The place seemed deserted. We decided to leave the path at that point and climb up the steep grassy bank that fronted the road.

# "A LUCKY ESCAPE OZ"

I scrambled up the slope by grabbing the long spindly grass, still wet and slippery from the early morning dew. On reaching the top, dense bushes separated us from the roadway. Although quite thick, they weren't too tall, about a metre high. We managed after some difficulty, to force them apart, allowing us to clamber through, but we were both badly scratched by the thorny bushes.

Stepping on to the road, I turned to the right and started to walk in that direction. At the same time, I could not believe my eyes. A feeling of horror and desperation overwhelmed me. About 100 metres away, walking towards us on the same side of the road, was the unmistakable figure of a German soldier. That drab grey uniform, I had not expected to see it quite so soon.

With my heart pounding, I momentarily stood still, completely stunned. Was our short spell of freedom about to end? I imagined that he must have seen us struggling through the thick, hedge-like growth. There was no time to talk and discuss the next step. It would look too obvious, turning round to walk the other way or running back into the forest. It would surely have given the game away.  All the time though, he was drawing nearer.  There was no alternative, we had to take a chance.  We must keep walking towards him, praying we could bluff our way out of trouble.

A few agonising moments later, we were just several paces apart.  He slowed his pace, I thought, "This is it!"  He was very tall, dark complexioned and of slim build.  I thought he was about the same age as me, a youth of about 20.  He wore the regular grey army uniform, with steel helmet and black leather boots.  He also carried a rifle, loosely slung over his right shoulder.

Looking me straight in the eyes, he stopped for a second and, speaking in a respectful manner, said quietly, "Guten Tag".  I could easily have reached out and touched him, we were so close.  I tried to appear calm, forcing a smile and returning his friendly greeting with a mumbled, "Guten Morgen".  Frank gave a sickly grin, nodding his head in acknowledgement.  I still wore my seaman's jersey and was glad he didn't realise the significance of the red letters NZSC on the front.

I felt apprehensive, thinking he was about to make conversation.  We would have had a severe problem if he'd spoken fluent French. Not wishing to give him the opportunity to talk, we didn't stop.  Instead, we casually strolled on our way.  To my immense relief, after a little hesitation, he also decided to do likewise.

A minute or so later, I thought it safe to look around. With my heart still beating madly, I half turned and peered over my left shoulder. I was relieved to see he had carried on at his steady pace. He looked neither left nor right, seeming oblivious to us and even less interested in his surroundings. I guessed he was bored with his everyday patrol, where nothing of interest ever happened. I thought he had seen us climbing through the bushes on to the road and was relieved when he failed to question us on our unusual approach. Dressed in our crumpled clothes and with our dishevelled appearance, perhaps he thought we were a couple of scruffy, destitute tramps. I watched gleefully as his long ungainly legs took him round a bend in the road and out of sight.

Frank looked at me and shook his head in disbelief, declaring, with a big smile, "That was a lucky escape Oz". I had to agree, and I said with a grin, "My prayers were answered Frank, I guess we were both born lucky. There must be more Jerries about, he won't be the only one. They could be billeted in houses in the nearby village, or maybe in barracks somewhere close by. We'll have to be more careful in future".

We now had time to take in the surroundings. It was getting much warmer, with the gradual rising of the sun. In the fields opposite, the odd farm worker could be seen. Close by, two dapple-grey horses were standing perfectly still. Penned in, they watched us intently over the sturdy wire fence that separated them from the road. Farther away, we could see a scattering of brown cows. Away to the left, was a sprawling, red roofed farmhouse with stables and a number of large dilapidated sheds. A green painted tractor could also be seen moving about in the distance.

It was early morning on a typical farm, an ordinary country scene, but one I really appreciated.

Aware of Germans in the area, we thought it safer to keep to the fields. The surrounding countryside appeared fairly flat. Dotted about were a number of tall, green trees swaying and rustling in a gentle breeze. Feeling exhausted through lack of sleep, we decided to approach a farmhouse to request food and shelter.

The street was still deserted, so we carefully climbed the high fence, making a safe landing on the soft earth below. We made our way across vast open fields, deciding whenever nearing a roadway, to keep closer to the tall hedges that abounded the area. That way we would be hidden from any German patrols or road traffic. Progress was much easier in comparison with tramping through the dense undergrowth and unyielding scrub of the forest.

It was still early morning, with the prospect of a fine Spring-like day ahead. With the French holidays occurring over the Easter period, it proved to be a fortunate for us. We navigated by turning Frank's watch with the number three facing the sun, number six would then be directly south. It gave a more accurate indication of the direction to take.

Walking at a slow steady pace, we discussed whether it best to sleep during the day, and walk at night, or do the opposite. However, we agreed to "play it by ear" for the moment, letting the fates decide. The immediate problem was to find somewhere for food and drink and have the deep sleep we badly needed. Extreme fatigue was beginning to take over as we trudged along. I could see that Frank's feet were very sore, although he never acknowledged it.

It was proving difficult to find a suitable place to seek help. We skirted a nearby busy farm, there were too many people around to take any risks. While in the camp at St. Medard, rumours circulated suggested the people of Northern France had no time for the occupying German forces. However, it was accepted some traitors and collaborators existed amongst the French, so with that thought in mind, we changed our original plan. Instead of just any farm, a more isolated one would be safer.

It was about 9.30am as we walked close to a hedge, alongside the road. Suddenly, there was the noisy roar of an approaching motor bike. Through the wide gates at the entrance to the field, I had an uninterrupted view. My heart missed a beat when I caught sight of the riders. Seated rigidly upright with eyes glued straight ahead, was the grey uniformed German driver, wearing a metal helmet and huge black rimmed goggles. Similarly dressed, seated in a very low sidecar, was his superior Officer.

Bluish coloured fumes belched from the smoking exhaust, as they chugged steadily along. Passing the large double gates, the Officer glanced in our direction. I held my breath. Would they stop and return to investigate? Thankfully, the loud throbbing noise of the engine slowly faded away. No doubt completely absorbed with their own thoughts and problems, they could hardly suspect an Australian and a Scotsman, two prisoners of war, were walking in the fields a few feet away.

I could breathe easily again. Having relied on our luck for the second time, we agreed to take even more care. If we became too tired, we could still enter the nearby forest to rest. No real progress had been made, but that was of little significance. We had all the time in the world. Our main objective was to avoid recapture by the enemy at all cost. I had no wish to be sent to Germany for the duration of the war. Also, the thought of reprisals or punishment was not pleasant.

Slowly rounding a gradual bend in the road, through the gaps in the trees, we saw a large village. We learned afterwards, it was Crespieres, situated approximately 20 miles west of Paris. Thinking Germans were probably billeted there, we were worried about safety. Deciding to make a detour of the area, we began to cross the field.

Walking towards us were two female figures. The elder one had grey hair. The other was a pretty, slim young girl, fair haired, with long wavy curls. Aged about 17,

161

we later discovered her name was Jacqueline Soubrier, in company with her Grandmother. We stopped for a moment and gave what I hoped was a friendly wave. We quickly decided to keep walking in their direction and met in the middle of the field. Not wishing to frighten them, I spoke in a soft voice, proclaiming "We are Anglais!"

On the 9th December 1997, Jacqueline, now a Grandmother herself, wrote to me, giving her impression of that meeting long ago, in 1941. I am honoured to quote from her letter.

# CHAPTER 9

## "WAS MUNSCHEN SIE"

## (WHAT DO YOU WANT?)

I lived with my family in Suresnes near Paris. As it was Easter time, I was spending my holidays with my Grandmother in Crespieres. Early one morning, we decided to go for a walk in the woods. Leaving the house, we crossed the main road and took a secondary road running to the forest. We were not very far from the village, when we saw two unknown young men, rather badly clothed.

We thought probably some poor country workers had left the forest and were coming towards us through the meadow. They seemed a bit hesitant when they arrived near and waved to us. The surprise! I thought I was dreaming when I heard them ask for something in English, but I didn't understand. For me it was exactly as if we had two Martians before us, because it was a long time ago that English people disappeared from our world.

As to my old Grandmother, she did not understand the situation. Being of German-Swiss nationality, she immediately answered them in the German language, saying "Was munschen sie" meaning. "What do you want?" This question, spoken in German, seemed to frighten the two young men. One plucked the other's sleeve, as if to get away in a hurry. I said excitedly to my Grandmother, "They are English!" After that short moment of panic, they explained they were prisoners of war in escape, but I don't remember their first question. However, whatever that was, we quickly decided to help them, as they seemed to be in very bad condition. We agreed it best to bring them discreetly back to our home.

That would not have been possible a few days earlier. A bedroom of my Grandmother had been requisitioned for a German Officer. Fortunately, he was now on leave in Germany, but he could come back from day to day. We did learn later, from the Officer's servant, that he had committed suicide whilst in Germany. However, there were still German troops stationed in the village.

My Grandmother lived as a tenant on a part of the farm. The owner of the farm was a lawyer, Monsieur Dounat, whose office was a room in a part of the buildings. The farm was managed by Madame Laurent, whose daughter Jacqueline was my best girl friend. We were inseparable, and always spent our time together. The situation was very dangerous for the four of us. It was important not to be noticed, so we returned home trying not to be seen.

*L-R:* E. SWEENEY, J. SOUBRIER, J. LAURENT, F. QUINN

165

The first thing we did on reaching the house safely was to give them some refreshment. Above all, I remembered they suffered very much from their feet, wounded by their long walk in bad shoes. Frank's feet were much worse than those of Edward. We helped to tend them, and gave each some slippers to wear. Edward was more talkative, open and resolute than his companion, who seemed a good fellow, but shyer, a bit sad and quiet. Of course, it was not possible to hide the facts of their presence from my friend Jacqueline, as she came to visit me all the time, as I did with her.

The son of Monsieur Dounat was her boyfriend, whom she later married. Her father and her two brothers worked in the Parisian suburb of Suresnes. They would return to Crespieres each weekend, also bringing some food for the week. All this is to say that there were soon several people in the secret.

My father was still at my home in Suresnes, where he worked in a factory manufacturing "Saurer" lorries. He was the maintenance department manager. On account of the seriousness of the situation, I had to inform him of the emergency. I realise now how rashly I acted in calling him from Ms Dounat's office, for the telephone was tapped by the German's. I announced to him directly, "Daddy, come quickly, we have two Englishmen!"

I remember vividly the first night my Grandmother and I were sleeping in the bedroom of the ground floor. We were awakened by Germans talking loudly on the main road, just outside the front of the house. Listening nervously to the sound of their voices, it seemed they had a problem. We were unable to see them, as the window shutters were closed. Immediately, it was feared they were in search of our two fugitives and perhaps they suspected our house. We never did know what it was about really, but after what seemed a terribly long time, they departed. Now, looking back, I suppose it was merely a night patrol, as there was a curfew from 10 o'clock at night, until 5 o'clock in the morning.

Early the next morning, my Mother and Father arrived as usual on their bicycles. They had cycled for about 20 miles. Although we had a car, there was no petrol available. Everyone was happy to meet the two Englishmen in such circumstances and we had a little feast to celebrate the event. At the time, my Father did not belong to the "Resistance". They were not yet organised and armed, although there were some individual incidents here and there. These were quickly followed by reprisals. However, it was sometimes rumoured that some secret channels helped people to leave the Occupied Zone and cross the Demarcation line.

On account of his profession, and also being a Freemason, my Father knew plenty of people and had the opportunity of contacting others, of whom he was not personally acquainted. Since the Armistice, the Germans had forbidden Freemasonry, but its members kept secret relations amongst themselves. I believe by this method, he quickly found the track of such a channel, after getting in touch with a neighbouring castle, the Chateau Millemont.

Edward and Frank stayed with us until Sunday morning, and I remember, before leaving, they made an agreement. If successful in reaching England, they would transmit us a message, "The Faraday has arrived". This was to be relayed during the news programmes, broadcast daily by the overseas service of the BBC Faraday was the name of the submarine that my Father served on during the time of the 1914-1918 World War.

Some weeks later, we were overjoyed when we actually heard the message and we gave thanks to God for their safe return home.

# THE CHATEAUX MILLEMONT

The suicide of the German Officer billeted with the family, was a very sad affair. However, it was cruel fate that such an unfortunate incident was to our advantage. During our stay with the Soubrier household, we were made extremely welcome, treated as though a part of their family. I felt secure and safe in their hands, knowing they could be trusted. Our good Samaritans' kindness and generosity did wonders for our morale.

Mdme Soubrier, whose name was Odette, seemed a jolly homely person. Jacqueline's parents were probably in their early forties. Even so, I had to admire their stamina and fortitude. A twenty mile bike ride from the Paris suburb of Suresnes to Crespieres under such worrying circumstances, must have been tough. For them it was a very precarious time, hiding two Englishmen in their home. Certainly, severe punishment of one form or another would be expected if we had been discovered. We realised the longer the stay, the more dangerous it would be for our hosts. After restful nights, sleeping soundly in a comfortable bed, I felt relaxed and keen to resume our travels. I enjoyed a good breakfast of croissants and coffee and later, bowls of hot soup for lunch.

Odette presented us with black berets and large shoulder bags. Each bag contained spare socks, bread rolls, biscuits and other items to sustain us for a few days. Sticking out of the top was a long stick loaf. I can still picture her face, when she said with a smile, "Now you'll look like Frenchmen going to work".

M. Soubrier kindly provided French francs, matches, and a few precious packets of cigarettes. We learned he'd made arrangements for us to receive assistance. The instructions were to go to the Chateau Millemont, a castle situated about 16 kilometres south-west of Crespieres. On reaching there, additional help would be available. The Chateau was jointly owned by relatives, namely Monsieur Begot and Monsieur de Baudus. During our conversation, it was mentioned Monsieur de Baudus was a friend of the French Consul in Liverpool.

In the meantime, we'd had some French lessons from Odette, learning to say, "We are escaped English prisoners of war". Regrettably, the time came to leave, but not before receiving some further advice. "Walk through the villages if necessary, but just act normal, as though you really are workers. In the smaller hamlets, people will know you are strangers, so take more care. Most villagers are pro-British though, hating Germans occupying their country. However, there is always the possibility of barracks nearby, with soldiers billeted in most villages".

We were sorry to leave, because although in danger themselves, it had not stopped them from sheltering us in our hour of need. There were a few hugs, some tears and handshakes. Then with warm cries of Bon Chance ringing in our ears, we waved our good-byes. Soon, we were walking along the road approaching the village. Turning round, we gave a final wave as they returned to their own difficult world once more. So began the next stage of our journey. We knew it could take several hours before we reached our next "port of call".

Millemont was in a south-westerly direction and we set off in an optimistic frame of mind. Frank's feet had healed and we both felt fit and ready to face any eventuality. Aware of Germans soldiers billeted in the village, we by-passed the area by keeping to the country lanes. We strode in a purposeful manner and, after about five hours, we approached the area of Millemont without further incident.

As we walked along the narrow country lane, on our left we came to the castle encircled by high walls. A large stately white building, with sprawling stables opposite, it stood in its own spacious grounds and was situated some distance from the roadway. The surrounding fawn coloured stone walls seemed to go on for ever. Overhanging was an abundant growth of trees and green leafy bushes. We eventually came to the impressive entrance. A pair of tall metal gates painted black and gold and securely locked, fronted the long driveway to the castle.

The place seemed deserted, not a soul to be seen. We stood by the gates for about five minutes, discussing our next move, when suddenly a tall distinguished looking gentleman emerged from the gatehouse. He asked a couple of questions, speaking slowly in French. I replied with our well rehearsed sentence, "We are escaped English prisoners". He shook hands warmly and in English exclaimed, "I've been expecting you".

He gave scant information about himself, except that he was the joint owner of the castle and a good friend of the French Consul in Liverpool. After relating our experiences to date, he reached in his pocket, took out his wallet and handed over some neatly folded French banknotes. He said with a wry smile, "You could try bribing the German and French guards if you're caught crossing the border. I will personally drive you about thirty kilometres in the direction of Tours, to help you on your way. You will have about 160 kilometres to walk before you actually reach Tours and later, the border of the so called Free France".

He told us of an address of a person to contact in the town of Pau in the south-west, close to the Spanish border. If we reached there safely, he promised a guide would be made available to assist in crossing the Pyranees. Climbing into his small car, I thanked him

CHATEAU MILLEMONT

profusely for his kindness, and agreed with his sardonic remark, "We'll all be in serious trouble if we're stopped by the Germans". After an hour of slow steady driving, we came to a halt upon reaching the outskirts of a very large populated area. He pointed out that it was the busy town of Chartres. Shaking hands vigorously, he wished us good luck for the rest of our journey. I had enjoyed the comfort of travelling by car, however, we were soon back to reality and on the march again, but all the while gaining in confidence.

# CHAPTER 10

## "YOU ARE GOING TO JAIL!"

Remembering the advice of Ms De Baudus and Ms Soubrier, we decided it best to walk along the main road sign-posted to Tours. They had suggested it would be less conspicuous and quicker than crossing farmland. Our plan was to travel by day and, if the weather allowed, to sleep in the fields at night. Under the shelter of hedges, we would be hidden from the roadway. By this method, we'd dodge the Germans on patrol with their dogs who enforcing the nightly curfews. Walking at a comfortable pace, the hours passed quickly as we strolled through several isolated hamlets.

Having exhausted our supply of food, on reaching a more densely populated area, we decided to ask for food and drink. Passing a small but busy cafe, the aroma of hot coffee was very tempting, but the premises were too crowded. Remembering the good receptions previously received, we thought it more prudent to approach the residents. We knocked on the doors of several cottages and did not think it unusual when there was no response. We noticed that, on occasions, curtains were parted and quickly closed again. One white-haired elderly gentleman did reply, but on hearing we were English, he abruptly slammed the door in our faces. I thought it very strange as he appeared to be quite afraid. I assumed it was our scruffy appearance that worried him. The reason would soon become obvious. Our presence had been made known to the occupying Germans.

On being unexpectedly rebuffed, we continued our steady walk through the empty main street of the village, soon reaching the outskirts. Suddenly two Gendarmes appeared ahead, running swiftly towards us. On getting close they roughly grabbed us by the arms. I immediately thought it was the end of our bid for freedom. It came as a surprise the way one of them said, softly and politely in perfect English with no trace of a French accent, "We are taking you to the jail!"

Looking furtively around, he said under his breath, "There are German soldiers billeted in the area, and they know you're in the village. They are methodically searching all the houses". He then said, "We have been asked to assist in the hunt. They are very thorough, but it is unlikely they will search the jail, you'll be safe there". I did feel rather suspicious though, thinking it was a ploy to make their arrest peacefully, then to escort us to prison without any struggle. I imagined we'd then be handed over to the Germans. The Gendarmes were both tall and well built, I didn't fancy our chances of overpowering them.

However, my eyes widened and the doubts in my mind eased a little, when he casually said, "Do you play cards, perhaps we could make a foursome?" Still holding us by the arms, they hustled us along at a fast pace until we reached a small isolated building; their headquarters. Inside, I noticed the heavy dark stained oak doors and imagined daunting cells behind them. There was no-one else on the premises, and we continued to be treated in a friendly manner. He insisted we would be safer there, rather than walking through the village. Although I still had misgivings being kept in the jail, they gradually faded as the time passed and the prospect of being handed over receded. I asked how he spoke English so well. Evidently, he'd worked for many years as a chef at the Ritz hotel in London. He allayed our fears even further when he said, "Don't worry, we will keep you here overnight and just before dawn, although there is a curfew, we can smuggle you out of the village".

For about an hour, he spoke of his experiences in London, and of the good times spent there. It was his ambition to return after the war. He listened intently to our story, which he translated to his colleague, but we prudently made no mention of our previous benefactors. During the course of the night, we played bridge, ate tasty cheeses and crusty bread, accompanied by mugs of steaming hot black coffee. It was inevitable that opinions would be voiced concerning the outcome of the war, with less than complimentary remarks and curses concerning

Adolph Hitler, his Luftwaffe Commander Hermann Goring, Himler, Goebels and his other Nazi cronies.

The Gendarmes had no love for the Germans. They obviously hated their country being under occupation, but under the present circumstances, were compelled to accept the situation. At least they could help us to escape capture, thereby frustrating and infuriating the German troops.

The hours soon passed and at about 4am, they decided it was time to leave. We gathered our few precious belongings and stepped outside into the cold dampness of the early misty morning. It was still quite dark as the two men led the way, telling us to keep about ten paces or so behind. On no account must we talk loudly for fear of being detected by the regular German patrols.

After about 15 minutes walk in complete silence, we came upon a narrow country lane. Speaking softly he said, "It is most unlikely you will meet any German troops on this route. It's a very quiet lane, eventually leading you back onto the main road to Tours". They both wished to remain anonymous, declining to give even their Christian names. It was becoming a habit thanking French people for their kindness and willingness to help, regardless of the consequences to themselves. As we said our thanks and goodbyes, as a joke, I whispered with a smile, "I'll see you at the Ritz Hotel, after the war".

The following days passed without incident. We slept in barns and fields, keeping a low profile. On one occasion we cadged a lift on the back of a farm wagon pulled by a huge cart-horse. Clopping slowly along, we could have walked faster, but for a few miles, it made a pleasant change just to sit and relax for a while. Eventually we jumped off the cart as it turned off the road and later approached a small isolated farmhouse, plucking up the courage to ask the woman occupant for food. Although she seemed rather wary, we offered some of our French francs in payment and were able to buy some milk and bread.

Since leaving Chartres, we had passed through several large populated areas, amongst them Chateaudun and Vendome. I did not mind the long hours of steady walking, as we often stopped at intervals for a short rest. Fortunately, Frank had no further problems with his feet and we were quite contented with our progress. Neither were we unduly worried about the time factor. Our journey was going well. It was great just being alive and not confined in a prison camp in Germany. Unfortunately, our freedom was not to last.

Nearing a narrow side road on our left, the unmistakeable aroma of coffee drifted in our direction. We investigated and found a small cafe a few yards away. Peering inside, I noticed there were no customers. One lone young girl, with long blonde hair, sat quietly behind a white marble topped counter. I guessed she was aged about twenty, completely engrossed in her book. There were very few people about, the street practically deserted so, being unable to resist the inviting aroma, we stepped inside the warm cosy premises.

Sitting at a small table by the window, with a good view of the road, we hungrily devoured hot croissants with our coffee. The girl, whose name was Marie, on learning we were English, had refused to take our French money. Not wishing to push our luck, we stayed only a few minutes. As we left, she gave a huge smile and presented us with two bottles of mineral water and a couple of fresh stick loaves to stow in our bags. It made our day. She gave us warning that there were many Germans billeted in the outlying district, on the border and in the town itself.

Continuing our walk along the main road, we passed through a small village, a few miles from Tours. Close by, large open fields were fronted by thick hedges, others were sectioned off with barbed wire fences. Locked wooden gates guarded an entrance to one field. A closer inspection revealed a muddy ditch running parallel to the road, about two metres further back from the hedge. As the night was drawing in, it seemed an ideal place to shelter, hidden from prying eyes. We climbed the gates, walked about twenty paces and settled down in our chosen positions, keeping close to the hedge.

Fortunately, the weather had been kind, with just a little rain occurring over the past few days. It was a calm still night when we were abruptly awakened by loud barking dogs which sounded rather too close for comfort.

Through the tiny gaps in the hedge, we saw two German soldiers approaching on the opposite side of the road. There were no street lights, and both men were carrying large flashlights, shining their long beams all around.

They were accompanied by two Alsatian dogs leading the way, straining on their leads. They must have sensed us. Frank said softly, "B***** Jerries", and dived into the ditch. I quickly followed suit. Lying in the mud and keeping our heads well below ground level, we kept perfectly still, praying we'd not be discovered. Anxious moments passed, but once again the gods were on our side. The noisy barking of the dogs faded in the distance, and then ceased completely, as the Germans continued their patrol.

With sighs of relief, we peeped over the edge of the ditch, making sure they really had disappeared. I grabbed a few handfuls of leaves from the hedge, in a vain attempt to clean the thick muck from soggy shoes, socks and clothes. In my muddy, baggy trousers, I was now not looking my best. We discussed whether to remain or to search for a more secluded place to hide. There would be other patrols in the area and anyone disobeying the night-time curfew would be challenged. Any attempt to run would undoubtedly bring a hail of bullets. We thought it advisable to stay put until the morning, when the curfew would be lifted.

Although well hidden from the road under the shelter of the thick hedge, it was impossible to relax. In the darkness, we decided to crawl deeper into the field, well away from the roadway. Sleep was out of the question though, as we mulled over another narrow escape. Eventually, after long anxious hours, we watched the first pale streaks of dawn appearing. They gradually widened, blotting out the darkness of the night skies. Thankfully, it was soon broad daylight and with the warm sun, I was in a better frame of mind once again.

The mud had dried on my clothes and I tried unsuccessfully to remove it. Looking so conspicuous, we decided to walk through the fields, keeping well away from the roadway and searched for somewhere to clean up. After a time, we came to a rather small farmhouse, close by was an old derelict wooden barn. We tried to gain entry to the barn, but the only door was barred and locked. Approaching the house, it seemed very quiet and appeared deserted. Frank knocked loudly on the heavy wooden front door, but there was no answer. Walking carefully round to the rear of the building, I used my fist to bang on the back door, but still no response.

There were no curtains and, on looking through the windows, we could see it was uninhabited and bare of furniture. Checking all the windows, one was unlocked but jammed tight and refused to budge. Frank hunted around and found some pieces of rusty metal. Using them as levers, after some difficulty, we managed to prise a small window open just far enough for us to clamber through.

A quick search upstairs revealed nothing, just a few large cobwebs hanging from the ceilings. On the ground floor was a spacious room, once a busy kitchen. Under the old-fashioned Butler type sink, was a mains tap. To our delight, on giving it a couple of turns the water, rusty at first, soon ran clear. Inside a large dusty wall cupboard were some old cloths, a towel, a half used bar of soap and a few rusty kitchen utensils, well past their best.

We removed our trousers, shirts, shoes and socks and rinsed off the dried mud. We took turns to stand in the sink, having a good wash down in the cool water. The front and rear doors were locked and heavily bolted. I had searched the cupboards for keys, to no avail. I climbed through the open window, with Frank handing me the wet clothes. These I laid out on the overgrown path leading to the house. The sun was quite warm and before long our clothes had dried. Meanwhile, we breakfasted on bread and cheese, washed down with mineral water. The downstairs stone floors were cold and uncomfortable. Being so isolated, we felt comparatively safe and were able to snatch a few hours of uninterrupted sleep, lying on the upstairs floorboards.

Our clothes had dried and eager to reach the border, we agreed to move on. We refilled our bottles before turning off the main supply making sure there were no drips from the tap. By not leaving signs of our short stay, we hoped to cover our tracks. Before leaving, we looked outside for signs of life, but the fields were deserted. After climbing through the gap, we ensured the window was tightly closed behind us.

We kept to the farmlands, but didn't lose sight of the roadway leading to Tours. The town was not too far from the border of Free France. I assumed we would also be free on reaching the unoccupied zone. Having been warned of the dangers so many times, it was expected to be the most hazardous part of our journey. Blue skies were turning grey, as heavy dark clouds formed overhead, blotting out the bright warm sun. It became very windy and overcast, it seemed stormy weather was approaching.

We passed several small farms, one in particular where a number of chickens strutted around pecking away in a large wired enclosure. I said to Frank, "I really fancy a nice boiled egg". Some farm labourers were working in the fields nearby. We casually walked up the cobble-stoned path leading to the ivy covered cottage. A plump homely looking woman, wearing a spotless white apron, appeared at the front entrance. She too was rather suspicious, but we succeeded in explaining our needs. We were invited inside, while four freshly laid eggs were hard boiled on the kitchen stove. After paying for some home made jam, fresh white bread, a large chunk of cheese and the eggs, we crammed the lot into our bulging shoulder bags and strolled contentedly on our way. At least now there was enough food to last for a day or two.

Later, the weather worsened slightly, bringing intermittent rain showers. Feeling confident and in good spirits, we had decided to take to the road again. It was quicker and easier than crossing the fields, particularly when the earth was wet and sticky after prolonged rainfalls. We made our way through the outskirts of Tours and eventually approached a very long and extremely wide bridge spanning the Loire river. Along the banks a few small boats were moored. There were no pedestrians to be seen, nor were any passing vehicles. The skies had darkened considerably, with black heavy clouds threatening more rain as we reached the bridge and began to cross.

# A SOGGY GERMAN ENCOUNTER

Walking briskly towards the opposite bank, I noticed a large wooden hut in the centre, on our side of the bridge. I assumed it was a builder's office, or something of that nature. Momentarily we slowed, almost stopping dead in our tracks. Two German soldiers emerged, awaiting our approach. My heart was in my mouth as they faced us, barring the way. Surely, they would be asking for our identity papers.

An agonising moment. With my heart now beating madly, we very slowly continued walking. I racked my brains for what to do? Should we turn and walk slowly back, or bluff our way through? Perhaps we could offer a bribe. Retracing our steps would have aroused their suspicions, probably culminating in an order to stop. There were only a few seconds to decide. We had discussed this kind of situation often, even thinking to claim to be American tourists on a hiking holiday. Without passports to prove it, we would be in trouble. I prayed out loud for help from above. I guessed there was only a short spell of freedom left. A prison camp in Germany seemed the likely outcome. There were just a few seconds in which to make a decision.

186

Our dilemma was quickly resolved, as my fervent prayers were answered. It was an unbelievable turn of events. A sudden bright bolt of lightning was immediately followed by a deafening clap of thunder. It was directly overhead. Almost simultaneously, a second huge flash struck, with the same explosive result.

The heavens opened up and obliged us with a torrential downpour. Huge raindrops splattered and splashed up again as they hit the ground with huge force. We were soaked to the skin within seconds. The heavy black clouds almost turned the day into night. Without a further glance in our direction, the Germans decided the shelter of their hut was the safest place. Not wishing to be saturated in the deluge, or perhaps being struck by lightning, they quickly disappeared inside, hurriedly slamming the door.

I said to Frank, "Run for it!", immediately making a dash across, ignoring the drenched German sentries as they peered through the rain splashed window. I shuddered with fear expecting gunfire, with a hail of bullets thudding into my back. I ran desperately as fast as my legs would carry me, until I reached the opposite bank. I glanced over my shoulder, but there was no sign of the Germans. I couldn't blame them for not being wishing to be exposed to that sudden violent storm. Rain was still falling heavily, but the thunder and lightning ceased. We just kept on running though, determined to put as much distance as possible between us and the sentries. Once well clear of the bridge, we took shelter from the cascading rain. It was a nerve-shattering few minutes and yet another narrow escape.

The weather gradually improved, with the dark clouds receding and fading in the distance. The sun shone once more, and with the clearer skies, it became warmer. We decided to get some help in either changing or drying our saturated clothes. After walking a few miles, we turned off along a narrow lane. At last, reaching open fields, we came across another small farmhouse. The owners were an elderly couple, and we repeated our only French phrase, "We are escaped English prisoners". The man, who possessed long white hair, seemed unperturbed at our soaked condition. Smiling, he nodded his head, indicating he understood, then beckoned us to enter their neat and homely cottage.

He spoke a little English and, along with a few odd French words we had picked up during our travels, we succeeded in conveying our story to date. Later, his kindly wife handed us warm blankets, insisting on drying our wet clothes near a large log fire. We took off our soaked shoes and socks and sat by the open hearth, wrapped in the blankets. It was warm and cosy as we sat and watched while she toasted bread by the fire's red hot embers. After a glass of home brewed red wine, with cheese and biscuits, we felt relaxed and gradually recovered from our earlier harrowing and exhausting experience.

Our clothes were soon dry, and nicely ironed. Later, he pointed out a small wooden barn at the rear where we could sleep overnight without being disturbed. He promised a good breakfast would be waiting next morning. Armed with blankets and pillows, we adjourned to the barn. Inside, at one end was a load of hay. We rearranged it in heaps until it was comfortable to lie on. By this time, we felt extremely tired, and fell into a deep untroubled sleep until early the next morning. Calling at the cottage again, we were greeted with a cheery welcome, accompanied by cups of hot fresh milk.

After a warm bath, followed by coffee and hot bread rolls smothered in home made strawberry jam, it was time to move on. We thanked them warmly for their help. Once again, without thinking of their own safety, we had been assisted by the caring, kindly French. By doing so, we knew they were putting their own lives at risk, as many found to their cost. Before leaving, they advised the border could be about 25 miles distant, depending on the exact route or direction taken. They suggested to keep to the fields when nearing the border. Unfortunately, that meant we wouldn't know exactly where the border was. Most farms had wire fences, many being sectioned off with barbed wire. The approach roads and bridges would have border checks with sentries and regular patrols assisted by the guard dogs. It seemed that the fields were the better prospect.

Our friends had thoughtfully given us a small map of France - a great help, but it didn't show the demarcation line.  There was some discussion and friendly argument between them, whilst, to the best of their knowledge, they finally pencilled in the border roughly where they thought it to be.  The map gave too little detail to be of any real significance.  Their suggestion was to head in a direction towards Chateauroux in the unoccupied zone.  From there, they advised us to catch a train travelling on the main line from Paris to Toulouse.  The 2000 year old picturesque city, was approximately just sixty miles from the Spanish border.  We thought it was a good idea, thinking that Toulouse was a safe haven, being so far south.

Our plan was to stay in the city for a few days and in the meantime, decide on our next move.  Who knew what might turn up?  In all probability, we would stick to our original plan of boarding a train travelling westwards to Pau,  a journey of at least 100 miles.  If all went well, we would meet our contact there, who would guide across the Pyranees into Spain.  Being an optimist, I thought it wouldn't be long before we'd be back home in the U.K.  The weather was fine and sunny as we tramped across the fields until we reached the main road.

While walking, occasionally we would see German soldiers in pairs, casually strolling along.  Other groups, numbering four or six men, walking in single file, were on normal patrol duties.  The latter were accompanied by Alsatian guard dogs.  We felt uneasy whenever they appeared, and would quickly take avoiding action.  We did not wish to meet them face to face.

Keen to reach Free France, we decided to walk throughout the night. Because of the curfew, we had taken to the fields again. From experience, we knew that under cover of darkness, there was less chance of detection from night patrols. Since parting company with Ms De Baudus near the town of Chartres, we had travelled approximately 80 miles. From Tours to Chateauroux, it was about another 60 miles, albeit "as the crow flies". Somewhere along the way, we would cross the border and gain our freedom, or so I thought.

After leaving Tours, we crossed the river Cher without problems. Our aim was to follow the Indre river to Loches and Chatillon, with a further 30 miles to reach our target Chateauroux. The following night, at one stage, I heard the barking of dogs. In the bright moonlight, we lay perfectly still in the long grass, as German guards swept their torches along their path. They were too close for comfort, only about 20 yards away. I held my breath as they marched slowly away from our hiding place. Gradually the torch lights faded in the distance and they were swallowed up in the darkness. At the time, not knowing our exact position, we thought nothing of the incident.

As daylight slowly approached, we came upon a small stream, with clear fast running water. Thankful for an opportunity of a rest, we had a good wash, ate some of our food store, followed by a long cool drink. It was a perfectly secluded spot and by now feeling very tired, we lay amongst trees and thick bushes, well hidden in the long undergrowth. Sleeping solidly for a few hours, we awoke feeling refreshed, looking forward to the next stage of our journey.

Keeping well away from populated areas, we had no further encounters. We eventually reached Chatillon and were amazed to learn we were actually in Free France at last. We had crossed the border without knowing it. I jumped up and down with joy and relief at the news and could hardly believe our luck. The patrol we previously encountered had obviously been at the border crossing. Nevertheless, at last we had finally achieved our freedom, or so we thought. But we were due for more shocks and further setbacks were in the offing.

That night we stayed at a small farmhouse and left early next morning. After a while, we again thumbed a lift in a farm wagon, travelling towards Chateauroux. At the station, we purchased tickets to Toulouse and as the train pulled slowly into the station, we could see a number of uniformed Germans sitting in the carriages. I felt distinctly uneasy as a couple alighted, more so when a few more emerged from a small waiting room. I was greatly surprised to see uniformed German soldiers in the Free Zone. I assumed they were on leave, seeing the sights.

Trying to appear casual, we made certain our chosen carriage had only civilian passengers inside. Feeling apprehensive during the long journey, I was enormously relieved when we arrived safely at Toulouse. We had been advised by Ms. De Baudus, of an organisation known as the American Society of Friends, where we would probably obtain assistance, should it be needed.

# "YOU'RE UNDER ARREST"

Twelve adventurous days had passed since our leap from the train. During that time, I often thought of my mother, who imagined I was still being held prisoner. I decided to write a letter as soon as possible, to give her the good news. We discreetly approached a middle aged woman in a cafe, telling her that we were Americans, and asked directions for the American Society of Friends. There we were met by a woman aged about fifty, who immediately warned us to be careful of the French Gendarmes. Many were traitors and could not to be trusted.

We were given shirts and socks and some French francs. I then wrote a short letter home, but she advised that although posted, it would probably be censored by the Vichy French authorities. That being the case, I did not write explaining the circumstances of our escape. I stated that I was safe and many months later, I learned much to my surprise that the letter had been delivered without censorship. As I had given my address as just "Toulouse", my mother couldn't work out what was happening.

After chatting for a short time, our American friend said we must leave. She seemed apprehensive and apologised for not being of greater assistance, explaining that they were under surveillance from the Germans. This was despite the fact that America did not declare war against Germany and Italy until eight months later, on December 11th 1941. I thanked her warmly for her kindness. We were obviously grateful for her assistance and with a change of clothes, felt less conspicuous. After hot milky coffee and thick slices of fruit cake, I felt restored. I was sorry having to leave, but there was no alternative. Although the Pyranees were not too far away, we decided to keep to our original plan. We would travel westward to Pau and meet our only contact. It was certain that he could be trusted. There was also the importance of having a guide to help in crossing the mountains into neutral Spain. I thought it our best chance of freedom.

Resuming our travels, we found the majority of French people, although wary at first of our motives, were very helpful. We stayed in farmhouses or barns overnight, and were not in any great hurry, being quite relaxed and assured. Steady progress was made over the next ten days, as we leisurely strolled towards our target. Everything seemed to be going smoothly when, early on the morning of the 6th May, we came upon a railway station. It was decided that we take a chance and risk catching a train to our destination, if only to give our tired legs a rest.

We purchased tickets, no questions were asked, and were soon on our way. Thinking of our safety, we agreed not to speak during the entire journey. Some time later, the train slowed and came to a stop, as we pulled alongside the platform at the bustling station of Tarbes. It was some twenty miles to Pau and, if all went well, we'd be on the final stage of our journey.

Our carriage was full, and we sat quietly with the other passengers, waiting patiently for the train to depart.

Suddenly, two armed Gendarmes entered and there was a curt demand for papers. I shook my head, explaining we were English. To my horror and disbelief, we were arrested and clapped in handcuffs. Other passengers watched curiously, appearing disinterested in what was going on, not wishing to be involved. I felt embarrassed rather than being annoyed at the turn of events. We were quickly bundled off the train, wondering what would happen next.

Marched hurriedly along the platform, we were taken to a small waiting room and thoroughly searched. Our bags were tipped out on the floor for inspection. Finding nothing of interest, we were ordered to repack our meagre belongings. The Gendarmes then held an earnest conversation with a rather officious looking person who had suddenly appeared on the scene. He didn't appear to be too concerned about our plight.

He was a tall man, middle-aged, wearing a smart dark grey suit. Despite our protestations demanding to be set free, we were completely ignored. He just looked at us with a disdainful stare. We hadn't the necessary papers to prove our nationality, and that was our problem, not his. Although the haughty bureaucrat had a good knowledge of the English language, he was not concerned with our story. We weren't told the result of the conversation, nor of their intentions. What with his uncompromising attitude, I feared that we might be handed back to the German authorities. A few minutes later, we were informed we were still under arrest.

They bundled us into a train and we passed quickly through many beautiful little villages. It was serene and peaceful as we watched the undulating green countryside of Southern France. It was obvious we were travelling eastwards as, in the far distance on our right, the tall peaks of the Pyranees could clearly be seen at times. We sat dejectedly and pondered on our destination. There was a little conversation with our guards, but they made no attempt to enlighten us. They were very friendly however, and agreed to remove our handcuffs.

We optimistically harboured thoughts of being taken to a lonely isolated spot, somewhere close to the French/Spanish border and then set free. Unfortunately, our hopes and dreams of Utopia were about to be shattered. It was late afternoon and with the sun still shining in a clear blue sky, we finally reached the small seaside village of Argeles-sur-Mer.

My hopes of freedom were dashed and our spirits plummeted when we were taken to another concentration camp with uniformed guards in attendance. Witnessing again the barbed wire fences and the drab accommodation blocks was a massive blow. I couldn't believe what was happening and just prayed it was only to be a temporary arrangement. Frank said in disbelief, "It reminds me of the camp at St. Medard, except the scenery is better".

Nearby were the azure blue seas of the Mediterranean with its unspoiled sandy shores. There was an awe-inspiring view of the Pyranees, now very close, but we had no time to look around, being marched hurriedly through the gates and handed over to our new captors. With smiles and strong handshakes, our escorts politely wished us "Bon Chance", and went on their way.

I asked for permission to speak to someone in authority, without success. Apart from one individual taking the usual particulars, date of birth, nationality etc., that was the limit of contact with anyone in a position of responsibility. The fact we were in "Free France" did not appear to be of any consequence, at least as far as we were concerned. I was feeling very angry at the latest turn of events.

# CHAPTER ELEVEN

## A FRENCH CONCENTRATION CAMP

In 1939, Argeles-sur-Mer was a small sleepy village in the Department (County) of Pyranees-Orientales, with a population of nearly 3,000 inhabitants. Situated on the sandy shores of the Mediterranean, it was approximately halfway between the busy town of Perpignan and the Spanish border. The County stretched high into the hills and mountains of the Pyranees, their splendour and magnificence towering above the Argelesiens.

It was during the final stages of the Spanish Civil war on January 26th 1939, that the Spanish town of Barcelona fell to General Franco's advancing armies. Towns closer to the border were captured as the Republican armies retreated. This resulted in an unprecedented attempt by thousands of Spaniards to cross into France.

The border had been closed, but by the 27th January, for humanitarian purposes, it was finally opened with the permission of the French Government. At first, only women, children and the elderly were allowed entry.

There was a massive build up at the border, and the roads were jammed solid with refugees. It wasn't long before the French authorities relented, allowing hundreds of thousands of escaping civilians and Republican soldiers to receive sanctuary in France.

Fleeing from the advancing troops of General Franco, many of these refugees were wounded, some with very severe injuries. Frightened people, including the elderly, little children and young women with babies, tearfully made the journey across the mountainous terrain. Most carried only a few precious belongings wrapped in a sheet or blanket. Accommodation was a major problem for the French authorities, and it was for this reason that the first internment camp was established in Argeles. The purpose was to provide an immediate form of shelter for the unfortunate refugees of many differing nationalities, although the vast majority were Spanish citizens. Being in close proximity to the border, Argeles was deemed to be the most suitable site. Consequently, a ten kilometre stretch of the sandy beach was selected for the position of the camp.

In the early days, refugees lived and slept on the sandy beaches. They were completely exposed to all weathers. Going to the toilet meant digging a small hole, which would subsequently covered over with sand. Although extremely tired and hungry, some would laboriously dig a large deep hole in which to sleep or shelter from the wind. Every day the numbers would escalate, as more dishevelled refugees arrived in their thousands.

Old pieces of wood and flotsam washed up on the beach would be used to build some form of cover as they endeavoured to escape from the bitterly cold weather. At night, the temperature would drop considerably. During the winter months, it was freezing cold, often with icy conditions. Some of the salvaged timber would then be used to light fires in an attempt to keep warm. Barbed wire fencing was erected all around the perimeter, penning in the growing multitude of refugees interned there. The erection of the fence resulted in a feeling of resentment amongst the Spanish. They felt they were being treated as prisoners, rather than refugees.

At one stage, nearly half a million people were crammed into this area, but the camps eventually became less crowded, as new ones were established. The number at Argeles was reduced from about 100,000 to 40,000. Providing suitable accommodation was a major problem. The French commenced building wooden huts, and portable latrines were provided.

At a later date, fresh running water was made available. One hut in the camp was converted into a hospital, to accommodate the sick and wounded. More serious cases were transferred to a hospital in Perpignan. Meanwhile, at Argeles, a cemetery was established close to the camp, for the burial of those who did not survive, for whatever reason.

The food ration was paltry, with a small portion of bread and a plate of watery soup twice a day, and coffee for breakfast in the morning. As the weeks and months passed, so the living conditions in the camps improved, but the problem of getting sufficient nourishing food was a never ending battle, with the numbers of refugees increasing daily.

At the outbreak of the Second World War, many thousands of Spanish Republicans joined the French army and the French Foreign Legion. Other men and women refugees laboured on farms and in factories, to help in the fight against the advancing German armies. The battle in France was lost however, as the Germans managed to overcome the strong resistance of the Allied forces.

Forced to retreat, most of the Allied soldiers were evacuated safely across the Channel from Dunkirk. Some 2,000 soldiers were left behind roaming the French countryside. Many were able to return to the UK, but some 50,000 men became prisoners of war. After fully occupying Northern France, the victorious Germans captured about 13,000 Spanish troops. These were transferred to a concentration camp at Mauthausen, Austria, and kept in captivity for the duration of the war, which finally ended in September 1945.

Meanwhile, back at the Argeles camp, we were searched, and our money again taken for "safekeeping". A couple of days passed and we begrudgingly settled in. A young swarthy looking guard, who spoke a little English, was rather talkative. I inquired whether there was an American Consulate, Red Cross, or some other organisation that might assist in obtaining our release. He promised to make some enquiries and, over the next few days, we patiently waited for an answer. Although gentle reminders were given, there was no still no answer. After a time, we gave up on the idea.

We had been imprisoned for two weeks and, despite constant demands for some information relating to our future, we were totally ignored. A further request to see the camp Commander came to nothing, and we began to get restless. The meals and conditions in the camp, although marginally better than Stalag 221, were still very bad.

We accepted that, in war-time, the countries involved would inevitably suffer a lack of certain foods. As in England, there was a shortage of most essential commodities, particularly meat and dairy produce. The German fighting forces and the armies of occupation had priority over civilians. For nine months now, our diet had consisted mainly of watery vegetable soup. Since our escape, with the assistance of several French people, we had on occasions dined on good wholesome food. I felt fortunate, keeping in good health and despite our problems due to the latest setback, we remained cheerful.

There was no news or signs of an impending release, nobody seemed interested, so we talked of escaping. From then on, the thought occupied my mind until it became an obsession. We talked of nothing else. We had no intention of staying in the camp for the duration of the war. The possibility that the Germans would take over Southern France at a later date could not be overlooked. We could be P.O.W's again, back to square one.

The mountains of the Pyranees looked positively inviting as we eagerly discussed our plans. Another option we considered was to follow the coast northwards, until reaching the French port of Marseilles. We could stowaway on board a ship of a friendly neutral country. Maybe we should try to reach Pau again, but omit the train journey.

Being so close to the Pyranees and the Spanish border, we agreed the most obvious choice was to cross at that point. Frank confirmed this when he said quietly, "If we're successful Oz, we might reach Gibraltar, with a passage back home to Scotland". His statement brought a smile to my face as I pictured the scene in my mind.

Although officially known as Francais Libre (Free France), there were many citizens throughout the whole of the country who collaborated with the Germans. They were widely known as quislings. The people living in the Free Zone were ruled by their own French Vichy Government. Many undercover German spies and members of the Gestapo were living throughout the so-called free areas. We had often been warned of their presence. It was common practice for young women to be punished by the patriots for fraternising with the occupying German troops. Their hair would be shaved off, identifying them as traitors to France.

In the Argeles camp, I was surprised to hear some interesting information from another prisoner. It was rumoured that guards, although carrying guns, had no ammunition. If this was the case, it would obviously be to our advantage. Whilst it was hard to believe, the possibility of the Germans forbidding the arming of the soldier guards was feasible. They would not wish to encourage a revolt by the French, however small it may be. Whether true or false, we would put it to the test. It was a calculated risk that had to be taken.

# THE MYSTERIOUS CUBAN AND A SECOND ESCAPE

One morning, while taking our usual walk around the perimeter, we met another person who seemed very friendly. On confidentially mentioning that we planned to escape, he guardedly and somewhat secretly remarked, "I have crossed the border many times". He didn't elaborate further, so I thought it unwise to question his reasons, whatever they might be.

He said he was Cuban and his name was Segura. At the time, he never divulged his Christian name, although he wrote to me at the end of the war. He was of medium height, dark haired and of slim build, with a fairly good knowledge of the English language. When questioned about his past, he always just shrugged his shoulders. I asked how he came to be in the camp at that particular time, but he declined to offer any explanation.

It came as a surprise when he suggested acting as our guide. Speaking very quietly, he confided, "I know the trails well". I couldn't disagree with the statement and was overjoyed at his offer. He recommended heading in

DEPARTEMENT
DES
PYRENEES-ORIENTALES
--------=--------
DIRECTION
DES
ARCHIVES DEPARTEMENTALES
----------◆----------

Perpignan, le 18 juillet 1997

## ATTESTATION

I the undersigned

Je soussignée, directeur des Archives départementales des Pyrénées-Orientales, atteste qu'un dossier provenant du service des étrangers de la préfecture, au nom de Edward SWEENEY , est conservé aux Archives départementales des Pyrénées-Orientales.

The information mentioned is the following
Les renseignements mentionnés sont les suivants :

Monsieur Edward SWEENEY
né(e) le 04-07-1920 à Melbourne
de nationalité australienne
a été interné(e) au camp de ARGELES-SUR-MER : arrivé le
06-05-1941 venant de Tarbes (Hautes-Pyrénées);
évadé le 22.05-1941.

Le Directeur des Archives Départementales
...
...

207

the direction of Figueras. If caught before reaching that town, people would normally be escorted back to the border and handed over to the French authorities. In all probability, we would then finish up back in Argeles camp where we started. Alternatively if arrested south of Figueras, we'd be taken to Barcelona for interrogation. Our plan was to reach Barcelona or Madrid and to contact the British Consulate. I couldn't see any drawbacks, but in the excitement of discussing our escape, we forgot we'd be entering the country illegally, without passports or visas. Spain being neutral, I couldn't imagine any difficulties.

The weather was becoming warmer each day. The hot sun in the cloudless blue skies beat down, although it remained extremely cold throughout the long dark nights. Our detention had so far lasted 15 days and I suggested to Frank it was time we made our move. We took a leisurely stroll around the outskirts of the camp, searching for a likely place for an escape, without being seen by the guards on the gates. We casually carried out our inspection and noticed a small gap in the wire fencing, an ideal spot, away from the gates. We decided the following day, the 22nd May 1941, would be our day of reckoning.

In the early afternoon, directly after lunch, we would go for it. Later we met Segura, showed him our escape point and arranged to meet him there at 12.30pm. At midday, we anxiously awaited the arrival of our hot soup and two slices of dry bread. Being hungry, we soon demolished our meal. I was feeling quite nervous and continued to think over our escape plan. One disadvantage was that we had no money or store of food, however, I thought that the lack of food would not really be a problem, as we had got used to the pangs of hunger by now. Apart from a noticeable loss of weight, we were still feeling fairly fit.

We had purposely planned our move at this time, knowing that many of the guards would be off duty, having their midday meal. We casually made our way towards the fence, keeping a wary lookout for the sentries on the main gates. Fortunately, at that particular moment, there were no others in sight. Frank whispered, "Quick, this is our chance", and grabbed hold of the wire. I was quickly alongside and we tugged together. The gap was soon large enough to scramble through.

We were watched by a wide-eyed group of prisoners, wondering what was going on. I glanced quickly around the camp, still no sign of the guards. It had taken only a matter of seconds to overcome the first obstacle. The inquisitive prisoners just stood around watching, keeping well away from the fence, not wishing to be seen to be involved.

I followed Frank through the gap, when there was a sudden rush behind me and I believe about five other prisoners also made a dash for it. I didn't stop to count them. Frank and Segura were already a little way ahead, trotting at a steady pace. Running swiftly trying to catch up, I expected to hear gunfire but not a sound was heard.

I looked back towards the camp. It was a relief to realise the guards were not giving chase. Just over five weeks ago, it had been a successful "Auf Wiedersehen" to the Germans. I hoped it would now be "Au Revoir" to the French for the last time.

The sight of the mountains looming in the distance ahead, gave us an added incentive to push steadily on. The more space between us and the camp, the better. We soon became breathless and slowed to a walking pace. Constantly looking behind, we checked to ensure we weren't being followed, still prepared to run or hide in the dense scrub and bushes if necessary. Segura stopped and said, "The distance to the border from Argeles by our indirect route is about twenty-two kilometres, and we have to keep moving". He thought we were not walking fast enough. He continued to lead the way, at a brisk walk, while we fell behind trying to keep pace.

After about an hour of scrambling through the dense undergrowth we became very tired. Some paths and tracks were really overgrown which made the going extremely hard indeed. Our guide said, "We must not walk along the main roads, you understand?" We accepted his advice, he was the one in charge. Keeping to the tracks was obviously the best way to remain undetected. It was also easier to take cover, if it became necessary.

We had travelled quite a few miles, when I heard the sound of running water. Rounding a bend in the trail, we

encountered a small, fast flowing stream.    Sweating
heavily and feeling exhausted and thirsty after our
exertions, we agreed to take a rest.    I knelt down and,
leaning over, had a long cool drink of the clear running
water.    Discarding my shoes, socks and rolling up my
trousers, I stepped gingerly into the ice cold water for a
quick paddle.

Later, as I sat resting my tired limbs, I watched the
swiftly flowing clear water becoming frothy and bubbly
as it negotiated the shiny wet rocks in its path.  It was like
being on a picnic, something I could only dream about.
Once I had stopped, I felt I could have stayed all day in
such an idyllic peaceful scene.    Time passed all too
quickly and after a stay of about 30 minutes, Segura
suggested it was time to leave.    Feeling cooler and
refreshed, we moved on.

Shortly afterwards, we began climbing up a long, green
grassy slope.    It was becoming more hilly with the
mountains ahead looming high in the sky.  Segura was in
front as usual, leading the way.   On reaching the top he
looked back and suddenly shouted, "Run into the bushes
and keep perfectly still!".   Glancing behind, slightly to
my right, I could see two Gendarmes on horseback.  They
were scrambling up a steep incline, headed in our
direction.  It was difficult to tell for certain, owing to the
winding trail.

They were still some distance away and as we lay hidden
in the scrub, I watched their approach.    They would

completely disappear from view, then reappear as they rounded the bends in the trail. Sometimes, all we saw were two heads bobbing up and down, as their mounts made their way through the thick undergrowth. I had a feeling of despair, thinking our attempt to escape was about to fail. We lay perfectly still, afraid to move a muscle.

A few agonising minutes passed, as we watched their inevitable progress towards our hiding place. They disappeared again for almost five minutes. Thinking that they may have given up the chase, Frank got to his feet, but our guide said softly, "Not yet, keep still". Sure enough, they reappeared, slowly negotiating another curve in the trail. All the time they were getting nearer to our hiding place.

We kept our heads down, peering anxiously through the scrub. I prayed there would be a detour and they would take another of the narrower trails that criss- crossed the area. As I watched them coming even closer, it seemed they must be in pursuit. We crawled deeper into the thick growth, hiding under very large bushes, some distance away from the nearby trail.

We couldn't know for certain whether we'd actually been seen. Segura suggested, if apprehended, we should split up and run in opposite directions. At least one or even two might possibly escape. After a quick discussion, Frank and I decided to stay together whatever happened. For a few minutes, we lay perfectly still, not daring to speak again. I couldn't believe my eyes, when about 200 metres from our position, they decided to discontinue their search.

Pulling back tightly on shortened reins, they turned their immaculate, sturdy horses round, negotiating the narrow winding path with extreme care. In single file, they trotted slowly back in the opposite direction. There were sighs of relief all round, as our faces lit up with broad smiles. I could scarcely contain my feelings. Yet another close shave! We thought it best to keep low for a while and waited about thirty minutes before moving on. Segura said our pursuers were probably wary of crossing the border and encroaching on Spanish territory. We continued our march across the mountains. It was hard going at times, climbing over the higher ground. Some of the larger peaks of the Pyranees reach a height of 10,000 feet.

Although late May, it was very humid. I was boiling hot and perspired freely during the day, but during the night, there was a complete contrast. I shivered in the bitter cold atmosphere, unable to keep warm. I'm not sure which was harder to bear. At one stage, Segura remarked we had crossed the border. I couldn't imagine how he'd arrived at that conclusion. I hadn't noticed any signs indicating we were in Spanish territory. All I could see were the lights from a few scattered farm cottages. He appeared to recognise the area. We accepted his word and were overjoyed at the news. Later, we were to experience entirely different emotions.

Upon reaching the brow of a hill, deep below us in the valley, was a pretty little village. As our money was in "safekeeping" at Argeles camp, Segura said he would go to the village, in an endeavour to obtain food and drink. "I shall be gone for a while", he said quietly, "But stay where you are, and keep under cover".

We never saw him again.

I don't know whether he was arrested, or if he returned to France, having successfully carried out his allotted task. However, after the war, I did receive a letter from him, dated the 30th November 1945. He was then working for the American Forces in Paris. Quoting, in his own words, he writes, "I suffer thousand misfortunes, but I don't lost my neck". He did not elaborate further, except to confirm he'd helped in our escape from the Argeles camp. Although I wrote asking many questions, I never received a reply. I still have his letter in my possession, but efforts to trace him have been unsuccessful. As far as I am concerned, the adventures and the mystery of the man Segura the Cuban, remains unsolved to this day.

After waiting hours for his return, we became anxious and decided to leave. By now we were hungry and thirsty. After walking wearily across the green hills, we discovered a small stream, trickling along its downward path. We drank greedily and refilled our empty bottles with the clear cool water. I tried eating grass and weeds to satisfy my hunger, but finding neither palatable, soon

Dear Edward
and family

A. Segura
3 B∘ KELERMAN
PARIS-13ᵉᵐᵉ
France
30-11-45

Dear friends

I hope hear
news, from you, now,
when the war
finish and everybody
are free

I suffer thousand
missfortunes, but I don't
lost my neck,

Now I am
working for U.S. army
in Paris, I am very well,
few days ago, I was
in the British consule,
and I ask, about your
he tell I must write to
you,

Regards to every
body,
YOUR obedient
Servant
A. Segura

215

P. L.
I, am the cuban
fellow who healp you
and anither fellows to
scape form angeles during
concentration camp
I think you will remember
of me,
Yours sincerely asegui

spat them out. We continued walking steadily, until we came across a small ramshackle wooden hut. Searching inside, it was empty except in one corner, there was a half filled sack containing what I thought might be bran.

Taking a few handfuls, I mixed it with water, and kneaded it into a flat shape. Lighting a small fire over a few rocks and placing the mixture on a flat stone, I attempted to bake the concoction. In the beginning, the fire started to smoke, so it was quickly doused to avoid attracting attention. On finding dry twigs and bracken, that problem was soon solved. I offered a hot stodgy lump to Frank, but he declined. It tasted terrible, but I managed to force down a few mouthfuls. Not long afterwards, I began to feel ill, as my stomach rejected its contents. I became violently sick. Fortunately, there were no further side effects.

Although hungry, we were in good spirits when we later came upon a few scattered farmhouses. Further afield in a valley, was a fairly large village and a chance to obtain some food. Making our way swiftly downhill, we came close to a number of cottages and were surprised at the sight of two burly uniformed men, suddenly emerging from a small nondescript building. They had evidently watched and bided their time, waiting patiently for us to approach.

Members of the Spanish Civil Guard, they were dressed in smart grey uniforms, with peaked caps bearing red headbands. Despite our protests, we were arrested, handcuffed and searched. I asked for food, but was told "Manana". Escorted to Figuares, we were interrogated and thoroughly searched, then taken to the local jail. Being in a neutral country, I had expected better treatment, not to be locked in a tiny stone walled prison cell. There were no toilet facilities, except for the use of the corner. Our constant demands for the Spanish authorities to contact the British Consulate did not seem to have much effect, nor did our repeated requests for food prove any more successful.

Later, still in handcuffs, we were put on a slow train, bound for Barcelona, situated on the Spanish east coast. While waiting on the platform, I noticed some orange peel that had been discarded. It had been well trampled, but I was past caring any more. I wiped it against my trouser leg, and the flattened dirty peel was hungrily swallowed.

Frank and I were shoved into a crowded carriage, watched by the other passengers. They whispered to one another and looked curiously in our direction. I felt like a criminal, as though I had committed a murder or some other heinous crime. Sitting opposite, was a pretty young girl, with long black hair. Aged about 16, she was accompanied by a middle aged woman, whom I assumed was her mother. The girl held a basket of shopping in her lap, with a glorious bunch of yellow ripe bananas protruding from the top. With my free hand, gesturing with my fingers to my lips, I said, "Ingles" then pointed to the mouth-watering fruit. She spoke quietly to her Mother, then with a sweet smile, she picked off two of the largest. I took them both with my free hand and passed one to Frank. The young girl's eyes widened and she stared at me with a surprised look. I had chewed and swallowed the skin, after greedily scoffing the ripe fruit.

I tried to make conversation to thank them, but our escorts intervened, forbidding me to speak. On reaching Barcelona main railway station, we were paraded through the busy streets, still handcuffed together. Shepherded into the nearby police station, we were locked in a small room, and later the never-ending questioning began. "What nationality", "Why no passport", "Don't you realise you have entered Spain illegally?". Again and again, "It is a serious offence." All statements and answers to the questions from our abrupt interrogator were methodically recorded - except one. The request I made to contact the British Consulate personally was ignored. A telephone call was an impossibility.

There was no food for us that day, we would have to wait for "manana".

The night was spent locked in a bare prison cell. The following morning, we were given a small tin of sardines. The instructions were not to eat it that day, it was for tomorrow. Later, in handcuffs, we were marched through the streets in full view of the public again. Nobody seemed to take much notice, I imagined it must have been a regular occurrence for the citizens of Barcelona. As wall as the inconvenience of being in handcuffs, it was a humiliating experience. In the late afternoon, we

BARCELONA - SPANISH PRISON

reached Saragossa, a very impressive town. Like Barcelona, it possessed many distinctive buildings, with some awe-inspiring features. Saragossa also boasts a huge bull-ring and is situated almost centrally between Madrid and Barcelona, roughly 240 kilometres from each.

The inside of the jail was not so good. Conditions, as with other Spanish prisons, were filthy, with little facilities for hygiene. Through the metal bars of my tiny cell, I witnessed a number of prisoners being beaten. I thought they were probably Republicans. They huddled together in a large group, with the prison guards wading in with their rifle butts. The weapons were used as clubs by gripping the barrel, with the butt end doing the damage. I don't know the reason for the attacks, I just felt sorry for the poor victims. I don't know if they had done something to deserve it, but this brutal punishment seemed inhuman. There was nothing I could do to alter the situation. Watching the incident, I thought it wise to keep quiet. I didn't fancy being on the receiving end of a beating like that.

Early next morning, I was actually glad when I handcuffed again, with the prison guards indicating we were about to leave Saragossa. Nobody spoke English, so there was no inkling of our destination. We had not been given any food or drink. We boarded another train, accompanied by two members of the Civil Guard, who steadfastly refused to remove the handcuffs. After travelling about 200 kilometres north-west, we reached the notorious concentration camp of Miranda de Ebro, in the Provence of Burgos, northern Spain.

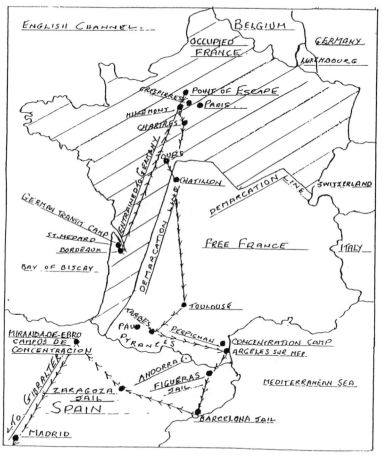

## ─ESCAPE ROUTE 1941─

ENGLISH CHANNEL

BELGIUM

OCCUPIED
FRANCE

GERMANY

LUXEMBOURG

PRESPIERES

POINT OF ESCAPE

MILLEMONT

PARIS

CHARTRES

TOURS

CHATILLON

DEMARCATION LINE

SWITZERLAND

GERMAN TRANSIT CAMP

ENTRAINED TO GERMANY

DEMARCATION LINE

ST.MEDARD

FREE FRANCE

ITALY

BORDEAUX

BAY OF BISCAY

TOULOUSE

TARBES

PAU

PERPIGNAN

PYRENEES

CONCENTRATION CAMP
ARGELES SUR MER.

MIRANDA-DE-EBRO
CAMPOS DE
CONCENTRACION

ANDORRA

GIBRALTAR

ZARAGOZA
JAIL

FIGUERAS
JAIL

MEDITERRANEAN SEA

SPAIN

BARCELONA JAIL

MADRID

223

# CHAPTER 12

## MIRANDA DEPOSITO DE CONCENTRACION

During the Spanish Civil war, many thousands of Republican soldiers and civilians were captured and became prisoners of war. This was a serious problem for the authorities, so an official order by General Franco's Government in July 1937, provided for the establishment of concentration camps. Prior to this order, buildings such as colleges, convents, universities and even large storage premises were utilised as prison accommodation. Paul Winzer, a member of the Gestapo and the SS arrived from Germany and was assigned to organise the building and running of the camps based on the methods used in Germany. Fortunately, this did not include the gas chambers used by the Germans to exterminate thousands of Jewish people, while Adolph Hitler was in power.

The Miranda camp was created very close to the river Bayos, near to the main Castejon-Bilbao railway in Northern Spain. The city of Miranda existed in ancient times and old documents suggest the name came from an Arabic word meaning Laurel. However, in Latin, the translation means Admirable or Wonderful. Unfortunately, neither of these descriptions applied. Miranda was also the name of one of William Shakespeare's characters in the "Tempest". Perhaps this was a more apt interpretation for the stormy times ahead.

Originally six wooden huts were erected to accommodate 4,000 prisoners. The total area was about 42,000 sq. metres. Many men were taken from Miranda and forced to work in slave gangs in the quarries nearby. It provided cheap labour for the Government. The prisoners also worked long hours in the construction of roads, bridges and railways. The restoration of war-damaged buildings throughout Spain was another task carried out by the weary prisoners.

Others laboured in Miranda camp itself, creating new buildings and providing other minor improvements. At the end of the Spanish Civil War, many of the soldiers captured were of the International Brigade. These brigades consisted of various nationalities including Canadians, Americans, English, Polish, Belgians, French and other Europeans. All these men were volunteers, although some were mercenaries fighting just for the money.

In June 1940, when France fell to the conquering German army, large numbers had fled across the Pyranees into Spain. Thousands were arrested by the Civil Guard and interned in Miranda, now the largest concentration camp in Spain. Due to the enormous number of prisoners involved, conditions became unbearable. Frank and I were soon to experience the terrible plight of the dispirited Spanish Republican soldiers and the unfortunate refugees, still interned in Miranda from the time of the Spanish Civil War.

We were marched into the camp, still in handcuffs, flanked by the two grumpy members of the Civil Guard. At either side of the open gate stood an armed Spanish soldier. They stood at ease, holding their rifles. I thought they looked decidedly scruffy and were a stark contrast to the smart, well-trained soldiers of the German army. I was glad when our escorts removed the handcuffs. When wearing them I always felt cowed, trapped and unable to defend myself.

Once inside the gates, we were approached by a young grim-faced Army Officer. I was appalled to see also in attendance, a swaggering, dark-skinned Sergeant, brandishing a whip. The long lash trailed behind him on the stony ground. I had the impression he seemed eager to show us how good he was with his whip. He ordered us by signs to stand to attention - a command we quickly obeyed.

The Officer wore a smart uniform, adorned with a row of medal ribbons. It was a the complete opposite of the dishevelled appearance of the Spanish soldiers. With some feelings of trepidation, we waited while our escorts were engrossed in a sombre conversation with the Officer. As they talked, the Sergeant glared at Frank for almost a minute, then switched his gaze to me. After a few seconds returning his stare, I thought it wise to ignore him and turned my head to look in another direction. I remembered witnessing the punishment meted out to the Republican prisoners in Saragossa. It would not have been unusual if we were about to receive a whipping. Who could tell what was in the minds of our brutal captors? A beating was a daunting prospect, one which we must try to avoid at all costs.

It was a glorious sunny day, beautiful blue skies, dotted with slowly drifting, snowy white clouds. As I looked around, my first impression was of the rows of dazzling white painted huts, glaring in the brightness of the hot sun. Dejected prisoners wandered aimlessly about, seemingly without purpose. Others sat in small groups, leaning against the walls of the huts, taking advantage of the shade. They appeared listless and preoccupied, showing no interest in the newest arrivals. No doubt they had observed these occasions many times before. The imprisoned Republicans were desolate, for they realised that there was little chance of their release within the foreseeable future.

After handing the Officer some papers concerning our previous interrogation, the Civil Guards gave a smart salute and strolled off, their mission completed. As they passed, they grinned and said in unison, "Adios Senors!"

Their behaviour made me worried about their intentions and it seemed a rather sinister remark.

A Spanish prisoner who spoke some English joined the group and we were put in his charge. He said abruptly, "I'm a cabo and you'll take orders from me". He was aged about 30, and a seedy looking character. I took an instant dislike to him and I'm sure it was mutual. My instincts told me he was a devious individual and my intuition later proved to be correct. We nicknamed him Pedro. Frank and I decided, as our own private joke, to call all the cabos by the same name.

They were mainly Republican prisoners, whom the camp Commandant thought could be trusted, enlisted as corporals as a reward for co-operating with the victorious Franco regime. Obviously all informers, they kept a sharp lookout for offenders. Irregularities would be reported to a sergeant, usually culminating in a severe beating for the unlucky culprit. The cabos reigned supreme, controlling the humdrum day to day running of the camp. Their word was law!

Having established his credentials, Pedro hustled us into a sparsely-furnished hut, loosely referred to as the administration quarters. There, a courteous Officer asked a few simple questions to confirm our story to date. Another person in a long white coat appeared, whom I took to be a medical orderly. On being asked to remove my shirt, doubts re-entered my mind. I thought of the bullying sergeants patrolling outside with their whips.

DEPÓSITO DE CONCENTRACIÓN DE MIRANDA DE EBRO

Apellidos............................................... Nombre..................

Prisionero en.......................................... Evacuado por..................

Natural de............................................. Provincia de..................

Profesión u oficio....................................

Estado........................ Esposa..................... Hijos..................

Edad........................ Filiación política

Talla........ Perímetro torácico........ Aspecto general..........

Cicatrices o tatuajes..................................

Color del pelo............... Ojos..................

Sano........... Pediculosis........... Acariosis..................

Blenorragia........... Sífilis........... Tuberculosis..................

Heridas de Guerra....................................

Otras enfermedades o afectos..................

Aptitud para el trabajo..................

Profilaxis............... Vacuna antivariólica..................

However, my fears were ungrounded, as we received just a cursory chest examination.

This was followed by two injections, one on either side of my chest. One jab to combat Typhoid fever, which is usually spread by infection from contaminated water. Many years ago, during the Boer war in South Africa, it was so prevalent, it accounted for more loss of life than the actual fighting. The second jab was to combat the threat of Typhus, which is associated with overcrowding and squalor. It can be spread by lice. Other forms of this fever can be caused by fleas, mice, ticks and rats.

Having completed his interrogation, the Officer handed me a registration certificate. It was headed Deposito de Concentracion of Miranda de Ebro and dated 26th May 1941. A few scribbled entries confirmed my place of birth, height, hair colouring etc., and that I was sano. I assumed this indicated I was sane, but the cabo later confirmed the translation actually meant healthy. Either way, I was pleased to be pronounced OK.

It was good to have that assurance, but I was deeply disappointed being imprisoned in a concentration camp for the third time. Whenever I asked for information concerning our release, the answer was always the same, "Manana!". On being dismissed, Pedro took over and escorted us to our hut. The wide entrance to the front and rear had no doors. There were some small openings in the walls devoid of glass. It allowed more daylight to penetrate and helped in the circulation of fresh air. I thought that was fine during the hot sweltering summer, but it would be a nightmare in wintry conditions. I wondered how long I would be imprisoned. A further escape might need to be considered.

The beds, if you could call them that, were just solid wooden boards, no pillows, no sheets and no blankets. Thick planks ran in a continuous line along one wall, with an identical unbroken row against the opposite wall. There were two tiers, just the same as the German transit camp at St. Medard, with a concrete pathway running through the middle. For those sleeping on the top tier, roughly hewn wooden blocks fixed to the posts aided the prisoners to climb aboard.

Frank sorted out two spaces together on the lower tier and claimed the space as ours. The other occupants were of mixed nationalities, but predominately Spanish Republicans. They spoke very little English, so there was no meaningful conversation. All wore identical fawn trousers, drab grey jackets, with peaked skull caps to match. On the front of the cap was the letter T, which stood for Trabajo, meaning worker.

Sitting on the bare boards, huddled close together, they looked withdrawn and dejected. This was the result of continuous heavy manual labour with little to occupy their minds. Freedom and being united once again with their families and friends was a distant dream. During all my time at the camp, I knew of no occasion when visitors were allowed any contact with the unhappy Spanish internees.

Pedro had left us to our own devices, but he shortly returned and issued us with lettered skull caps, spoons, and battered tin bowls. Having eaten very little over the past few days, we agreed that whatever was on the menu would be just fine. This was just as well, bearing in mind the quality and condition of the food we later received.

The Cabo glared at us in turn and said, "There will be a bowl of black coffee for breakfast, and two meals a day. No second helpings, neither will you get coffee at any other time. At meal times you will hear the bugle call, and assemble quietly on the parade ground". Frank turned to me saying hopefully, "It sounds promising to me Oz, I can hardly wait for the sound of that bugle". As he left, Pedro's parting shot was, "It is forbidden to leave the hut after eight p.m. If you need to go to the toilet during the night, don't wear trousers. If you do, you will be fired on". That shut us up.

At last there came the eagerly awaited sound of the bugle. It resulted in a rush of jostling bodies forming two long queues in single file. Cabos were in attendance to ensure a more orderly approach. Others stood behind the steaming hot containers pouring a full ladle into each person's bowl. Each pan was about three feet in diameter, with an approximate depth of twelve inches. Two Sergeants gripping their whips, stood menacingly to one side, ready for any signs of trouble. The sergeant at the head of my queue, had a very pronounced limp. It was said to be the result of injuries received during the Civil war. As well as a whip, he possessed a heavy knotted walking stick, which to my great discomfort, I would soon be acquainted with.

The soup consisted mainly of very large bean skins, similar to broad beans, but twice the size. Pedro called them horse beans. The liquid was black and gritty, it was obvious they had not been washed and no care was taken over the preparation. Another talkative cabo mentioned that most of the beans were separated beforehand and fed to the soldiers. We were left with the skins and the dirty liquid. Probably the skins were just as nutritious as the beans. Pity they were not washed first though.

I had earlier taken a walk around the site, and came across a pile of rubbish awaiting collection. Having very few qualms by this time, I rummaged about, turning the pile over with my foot, hoping to find something that might be useful. The smell of rubbish and kitchen waste soon got the better of me, but I had discovered a battered tin bowl, identical to our meal dish. A plan to gain extra food hatched in my mind. I cleaned it with a piece of rag, took it back to the hut and hid it out of sight.

On reaching the head of the soup queue, I received my ration. Still desperately underfed, I decided to put my plan into action. I walked slowly and furtively back to the hut and the bowlful was quickly emptied into my previous find. A slow walk to the hungry queue was called for, so it was done with a show of nonchalance. I hoped to remain unobserved. I then rejoined the still lengthy queue, feeling like Oliver Twist. It seemed my scheme was working well, and the crucial moment eventually arrived.

I leaned over slightly, with my right arm out-stretched hoping to receive my second helping. Unfortunately, the Sergeant had other ideas. Without warning, he struck a heavy blow across the back of my neck. It was forcefully applied with his gnarled walking stick. Although not an exceptionally well-built man, he certainly put plenty of power into the strike and I collapsed on to the ground. I cried out loudly with the pain, and stayed still for a moment or two, expecting further punishment Fortunately, there was none. I was thankful he hadn't used his whip too, which was held in his other hand.

Frank, witnessing my unsuccessful attempt to obtain an extra portion, quickly ran to my assistance and with the aid of another prisoner, escorted me back to my hut. I was laid flat on my back on the hard boards. The pain was excruciating, and I called the sergeant a few choice names. Luckily, he was not close enough to have heard me question his parentage. Despite the massive impact from the stick, I soon recovered apart from a few colourful bruises and a stiff neck for a few days. There were no further repercussions, but a painful lesson was learnt. My endeavours to obtain a second helping would definitely not be attempted a second time.

# I SALUTE GENERAL FRANCO

In the late afternoon before sunset, the bugle sounded. It was time to pay our respects to Spain. We obediently assembled on the parade ground to kow-tow to General Franco and the Spanish flag. On a large wooden platform, alongside the flagpole, stood the imposing figure of the Camp Commandant. He was accompanied by two soldiers and a junior Officer. The raised structure gave a good view of all the prisoners, as we stood to attention, silently waiting for the ceremony to begin. The silence was assured by the presence of the Sergeants displaying their whips.

As the flag was lowered the Commandant gave a smart salute. This was followed by loud proclamations in Spanish. In reply, all prisoners were compelled to repeat and shout loudly, "Arriba Espania" or "Viva Franco", whenever the occasion demanded. Repeatedly, we were compelled to give the Fascist salute by fully extending our right arms high in the air, as we sang the national anthem, "Arriba Espania", and General Franco's hymn, "Cara El Sol".

Watchful Sergeants trailing their whips, walked between the rows of prisoners, to ensure the ceremonies were carried out with due respect. The occasional loud cracking of the whips was an visible reminder of the consequences of any sign of disobedience. Regardless of this threat, it did not deter the British contingent from shouting out loudly and with intense feeling, a rather less complementary substitution. "Arriba Franco" became "**** Franco". Fortunately, the cries of the British were drowned by the thunderous shouting of the remainder of the prisoners. However, the vehement expression used gave some satisfaction as well as amusement, helping to relieve the feelings of tension, frustration and hatred. The ceremonies were held twice daily. Firstly with the flying of the flag in the morning, and further salutations when lowered in the early evening.

The rendering of the national anthem at the ending of each parade was accompanied by a military band. I found the music very pleasant and enjoyed the experience. Not having heard any music for almost a year, I thought how wonderful it sounded. The end of the National Anthem signalled our dismissal. One or two prisoners would then receive a quick flick of the whip for no reason, except as a pre-emptive warning. Vacating the parade ground had to be carried out in complete silence and in an orderly manner. It was wise to obey these commands.

As we walked slowly towards our hut, we were approached by another Republican prisoner proclaiming, "I'm the camp barber". We had been warned by another cabo to expect this procedure. Producing his clippers, he made a single cut from the back of my neck to the top of my forehead. Frank was treated in the same way. He then advised, "If your hair is not fully shaved off by the following evening's parade, you will be severely punished". As I had no intention of incurring the wrath of the Sergeants and the prospect of a whipping, I made sure the order was obeyed early next morning.

Some prisoners thought the removal of a person's hair was meant as a humiliation, or perhaps to make it harder for an escapee to go unrecognised. To me it was useful to ward off the many insects and bugs that prevailed in the camp. Unfortunately, it was a futile attempt, for the close cropping of the hair with clippers did little to deter the head lice. I thought it a better solution to shave off all the hair with a razor, although I wasn't too keen on the prospect of being completely bald.

On the very first night I experienced the hopeless fight against the relentless fleas and lice. Having been thoroughly bitten and finding it impossible to sleep, I removed my shirt, to kill some of the little blighters. Along with the rest of the prisoners, I continued to scratch the annoying itches, but my body was almost completely covered with bites. Later, I got some relief and after a close inspection, I put my shirt back on and attempt to doze off. After a short time, more insects infested my clothes and I was bitten again. It was a constant battle, one I could not win. During the day, the itching was almost bearable. Every night though, the routine was repeated, continually scratching and hunting for the attacking hordes. Although the Spaniards were obviously aware of the situation, no effort was made to destroy the pests. I must admit I never had that problem in the German and French camps.

I soon became infected with crab lice and in an attempt to cure the problem, I shaved the hair from my body. I also suffered a severe attack of dysentery, for which there was no treatment available. The only solution was to go without bean-skins for a few days. Unlike the camp at St. Medard, no running water was available inside the huts. Sturdy troughs of clean water stood outside, supervised under the ever-watchful gaze of the cabos. Woe betide anyone who misused the clean water in any way. A beating was guaranteed to follow.

On occasions we were forced to bathe in the clear flowing waters of the river that ran at the far end of the camp. The evil sergeants, cracking their whips, ensured there were no laggards. The hated cabos ran in and out of the huts, urging everyone, without exception, to rush down to the river's edge. We ran through an opened gate flanked by two unkempt Spanish guards. Lounging lazily against the thick wooden posts, they watched with sardonic grins, as we scrambled down the green grassy bank leading to the river. The main railway lines were quite close on the opposite bank, running in a parallel direction to the campsite. It was compulsory to bathe in full view of the passing passenger trains.

The water was invariably very cold, and diving in took my breath away. Not having the luxury of swimming costumes, there was no alternative but to bathe in the nude. I ignored the passing rail traffic, as nobody seemed to care. Swimming without clothes was actually a major advantage, as it washed off any remaining insects and eggs from my body. It also completely curtailed the itching for a time, although the insects would return each night for their regular feed.

# "THERE'S SOMEONE TO SEE YOU"

A grinning Pedro later entered the hut with exciting news. "Go to the administration hut, there is someone to see you". At last there was a visit by the Assistant Naval Attache from the Embassy in Madrid. It was our first meeting with a British official since our escapes. The fact that the Consulate was now aware of our existence was reassuring. Our future seemed much brighter. It meant our relatives would be informed of our safety. However, I was still confined in the largest concentration camp in Spain. At least 3,000 to 4,000 men were imprisoned there at any one time, having to suffer the barbaric conditions that had existed since the camp was first established in 1939.

I had previously discussed with Frank the possibility of another escape, with the aim of reaching Gibraltar. However, we decided against the idea, when a cabo informed us of two previous unsuccessful attempts. It was alleged that a party of eight Polish prisoners were shot dead in one failed bid. On another occasion, a recaptured prisoner was alleged to have been tied to the flagpole and left overnight in the freezing cold weather. Next morning he was found dead. The body was left bound to the flagpole for a long time, as a deterrent to others. I didn't fancy our chances of escaping from Miranda, due to the dire consequences if caught.

However, we were pleased to meet the Attache, and during the interview, I enquired about the Spaniards' intentions regarding our imprisonment. He gave the news we longed to hear. "You will eventually be released and allowed to return to Britain. Spain is a neutral country, and they have no legal right to detain you. Once your nationality is proved your release will be granted".

When we asked how long that would take, he answered guardedly, "Unfortunately, it is not our decision, it could be weeks or months. It is entirely up to the Spanish authorities. The Consulate can exert some pressure, but it is a diplomatic problem which must be handled with care and patience". He then added, "Please tell me all you can about the Black Raider. Even the smallest item could be of significance".

He took a small black notebook from his leather brief case and jotted down only items of interest, events that occurred during our time on the German raider. The routes taken, meetings with other German vessels, how and where they were supplied, all could be of great help. I hoped our scant information would be of some real assistance to the Admiralty in their efforts to apprehend the German ships. Upon leaving, he mentioned there would be a visit from the British Consulate, when we'd be given some assistance, namely a little tinned food, cigarettes and a limited amount of money. The interview was all too soon concluded, but I was elated at the news of our impending release.

Gossip circulating amongst the prisoners, suggested that General Franco did not wish to be seen to favour the British by appearing to give them preferential treatment. Evidently he was afraid of Adolph Hitler's future intentions. With the might of the all powerful Germany army, there could easily be an occupation of the whole of France, instead of a part. This could then be followed by an invasion of Spain. Under the circumstances, Franco was very diplomatic where Britain and Germany were concerned, particularly with regard to the British escapees. He was in an awkward situation, not wishing to upset either power.

It was on June 3rd, 1940, that the final evacuation from Dunkirk took place, when approximately 20,000 British soldiers were left behind. Most of these survivors were captured and spent the duration of the war in German prison camps. Those who managed to evade German search parties, reached England by various means, often with the help of the French people. The main escape route meant crossing the Pyranees into Spain. In the attempt, many were arrested by the Civil Guard and interned in Miranda. Eventually, they would be released and returned to Britain.

Including Frank and myself, confined in the camp were approximately fifty British prisoners, a mixture of soldiers, R.A.F personal and twelve merchant seamen. The latter had escaped from various trains en route to

242

Germany. Of the few airmen who survived after being shot down over enemy territory, some managed to cross into Spain, where they were arrested. There was very little contact, conversation or comradeship amongst the British prisoners. Despite us all enduring the same hardships, no lasting friendships were made.

As on the German ships, there were no newspapers, radios, books, cards, or board-games. No form of entertainment was organised to assuage the terrible conditions. Our only topic of discussion was the question of the release, if and when it would take place. There was little else to discuss. My sole valuable possession was a gold ring I was wearing at the time of the Orion's attack. It was given to me by a young girl named Miriam Ronneberg, whom I met in New York, before beginning the fateful journey to Australia. She was very beautiful, with long blonde hair. We'd had a wonderful time seeing the sights, visiting Times Square and taking the ferry to Staten Island. Being ravenously hungry in the Miranda camp, I had exchanged her ring with Pedro for a small bread roll. I lost Miriam's address when the ship was sent to the bottom of the sea with the rest of my belongings. Over the years I made several attempts to trace her, to no avail. Although I felt terribly guilty at the time, I am certain she would have forgiven me, considering the dire circumstances.

Officers appeared to be treated more favourably by the Spaniards. Most were accommodated in their own quarters, segregated from other ranks. On occasions, their soup was delivered to the hut in bulk. It enabled them to avoid the rush and queues that formed at meal times. However, their staple diet was no different to mine. A further concession to Officers was made when issued with parole cards. It freely allowed unaccompanied visits to the town centre. I asked a cabo to request similar treatment for Frank and myself. Later he returned with the answer, a point blank refusal. I thought about it and concluded that perhaps our track record of escapes went against us.

Better news at last though, when the British Military Attache, Lt. Colonel Drummond-Wolfe arrived. His timely visit resulted in weekly payments of £1.00 cash, and a packet of ten "Players" cigarettes per week for each person. Also to be shared out, were some small food items, such as tinned fish, corned beef and packets of biscuits and cheese. The food had to last for two weeks, when another ration would be issued.

We pressed him for information regarding our release but he had no further news. We just had to let matters take their course. He advised us to keep out of trouble and not aggravate the Spaniards in any way. I had no intention of ignoring that particular piece of advice. A beating and a spell in the "Calabozo" was the last thing I needed. At some future date, if all went according to plan, we would be taken to Gibraltar, and shipped home to Britain. Like the other prisoners, I had to bide my time and obey my masters without question.

# BUILDING A SPANISH ROAD

Early the following morning, Pedro sidled up close alongside. There was a smirk on his swarthy face as he said, "Good morning, I'm putting you to work on the stones today". I asked what that meant. He replied with a sneer, "You will soon find out, don't forget, be at the gate within thirty minutes, don't be late".

I wondered was going on. Before I could question him, he abruptly said, "Adios Senor", then wandered off, disappearing into the next hut. Shortly afterwards, a noisy, rusty open truck, with beige painted metal sides approached. It pulled up in the roadway just outside the camp. With loud shouts of "Idese prisa!" (hurry up) from the cabo, we were hustled through the open gateway. The two armed soldiers faced each other at either side of the wide entrance. They stood at ease, as usual, armed with rifles. I nodded my head towards the sentries in acknowledgement, as they bid "Beunos Dias"

Wearing my worker's grey cap and prison clothes, (about two sizes too large), along with a number of young Republican prisoners, we scrambled on board, accompanied by two scruffy guards. We obediently sat with legs crossed, huddled together on the dusty metal floor. One guard, with a cigarette dangling from his lips, propped himself against the back of the driver's cab, while the other perched precariously on the truck's side. A third soldier sat in the cab, accompanying the driver.

A young Spanish prisoner, who looked about the same age as me, sat by my side. He informed me that we would be helping with the building of the new road. After a short bumpy journey, travelling at high speed, we reached an open area, where I saw piles of large stones. I understand that they had been transported from the nearby quarries, the first in the vicinity of Pobes, with a second at Nanclares De Oca, in Alava Province. The Nanclares quarry was approximately seven miles from the Miranda camp.

On jumping down from the tailboard, I was handed a large circular wicker basket, with short rigid handles on opposite sides. It measured approximately 50cm across, and about 30cms in depth. I was ordered to join a line of prisoners each carrying a basket. With armed guards standing close by, two Republicans, using their hands, filled each basket to the brim. At a sign from the guards, the prisoners grabbed hold by the handles, and in one single movement, the load was heaved and placed across my shoulders.

Escorted by another guard. I walked unsteadily for about forty metres. My head and shoulders were bent forward, with my back feeling the strain. On reaching the roadworks, two men lifted the container from my aching back. The stones were then tipped out to form a base for the new road. There was a brief respite, while freshly dug earth was shovelled into my basket. It proved to weigh heavier than the stones. Urged on by the guards, I struggled slowly back to the starting point, where the load was removed. This back-breaking, hot and dusty procedure was repeated many times over. Back and forth in the heat and with June and the scorching hot, humid summer still to come, I was not looking forward to long spells of hard labour. In the beginning, at least it was a change of scenery, getting away from the camp. However, after my first spell of road making, I was glad when it was time to return to my hut and rest my weary limbs.

I have always been strong willed, able to cope with most things, but working on the stones was utterly soul destroying. The most physically draining work imaginable, my back and legs throbbed and ached, and my shoulders were agony. After a few hours non stop, we were driven back to the camp for our quota of bean skins and fortunately, did not return again that day. I would be reaching my 21st birthday on July 4th, and road making would not be the best way to celebrate it. I thought I'd persevere for a few days while I decided on some plan of action.

After seven days of gruelling punishment, I'd had enough. I thought I'd tackle Pedro about my problem. I suspected that a bribe might work, maybe that was what he hoped for anyway. After the conclusion of the saluting ceremony, I approached him and said meekly, "My back is killing me, the work is too heavy. I can't stand it any longer. What can you do about it?" He was aware we'd received our food parcels from the Consulate, so with a smile, I offered him half of my meagre cigarette ration and a small tin of salmon. He readily agreed, but I knew he'd be back for more, once I'd received my next issue. With a slimy smile on his weather beaten face he said, "I'll put both you and Frank on the rubbish cart".

He added, "It will be your job to keep the camp site tidy. Any problems from either of you, you'll find yourselves back on the stones". I didn't mind clearing up the rubbish with a hard broom and shovel, anything was better than the roads. I felt certain that forcing us to slog away on the new road was his own crafty little scam. It was his way of getting his greedy hands on our meagre supplies, particularly the cigarettes.

He'd already deprived me of my precious gold ring, but I could hardly blame him for that. Being so hungry, I had accepted his offer of exchange. The bread roll was the best deal I could get. It was as simple as that. However, that was yet another reason why I considered him devious, and not to be trusted. My intuitive impression on the very first day had subsequently been proved correct. Although a prisoner himself, he had the upper hand, and could act as he wished to satisfy his own needs. The large wooden rubbish cart possessed two long shafts. When I first saw it, I had imagined that a couple of harnessed horses towed it around the camp. I never thought I'd enjoy collecting rubbish and waste, but anything was better than the hard labour of the previous seven days.

Over the next few monotonous weeks, we kept a low profile, carrying out cleaning duties. Inside the camp, the humdrum routine and conditions remained the same. Twice a day, we joined in the loud chorus of "Viva Espania" and "Viva Franco". Each night, the scratching and the hunt for the hordes of biting insects continued unabated. Pedro received his weekly cigarette ration from us, so he was happy. I was in a better frame of mind, no longer involved in road building. The barber had cut a path through the centre of my hair again. Because of the usual threat of a severe beating from a Sergeant, the following morning my hair was clipped off for the second time.

Rumours were spreading that there would soon be a release for all the British. After almost a year of being a prisoner and on the run, it seemed repatriation may not be far off. Could it be true? I longed and prayed for the day when I could say "Adios Senors", and really mean it.

At last, my prayers were answered. The news circulated from the Consulate official that we were among those being released. After ten weeks of sheer humiliation and degradation, I couldn't believe it was about to happen. No longer a member of the working party, I handed my prison outfit to the cabo, reverting again to normal every day wear.  Although most of my clothes were well worn, it was better then wearing the prison uniform.  The following day, as I was leaving, Pedro   approached, shook hands and wished me good luck.  I wasn't sorry to see the back of him though, or the last of the brutal Spanish sergeants.

In the 1960's, the Miranda concentration camp was demolished, leaving no sign it ever existed.  In its place, there now stands a huge block of offices, belonging to the Elf Oil Company, now under part French Government ownership.  To this day, just like a pilgrimage, people from many countries from all parts of the world visit the site with their families.  All have there own personal memories of the degradation suffered in Miranda.  Some unfortunate men would have spent many years imprisoned in the infamous camp, before their release was finally granted.

My own personal experiences during the war and, finally, the humiliations endured in Miranda Campos De Concentracion, are firmly engraved in my memory forever.  Even with the passage of time, the traumatic events have not been dimmed in my mind.

# THE ROCK OF GIBRALTAR

On August 5th, after a long tedious route via Madrid, we crossed La Linea, dividing Gibraltar and the Spanish mainland. It was a euphoric feeling as I passed through the checkpoints. I watched the happy faces of people walking freely round the busy streets and shops. Seeing policemen dressed in uniforms identical to our English "bobby", was a comforting sight to behold. The scene could have been of any town in Britain. It brought back fond memories, and I yearned to be home once again. Since leaving Britain, there had been many months of frustration. I could hardly believe it was nearly over.

We were taken to a small hotel and enjoyed the luxury of a good soak in a blissful bath full to the brim with very hot water. Later we adjourned to the dining room, where a typical British meal was served. Fish and chips, side salad, fruit and ice cream, and a glass of chilled white wine was the feast we were served. Frank said afterwards, it was fit for a king. I heartily agreed. I'd forgotten how delicious fried fish and greasy chips could taste.

New clothes were provided at a nearby gents' outfitters. It was a dream come true. After carefully choosing a

251

complete set of clothes, I felt a different person, at last I was able to take some pride in my appearance. Being extremely self-conscious about my shaven head, I decided on a bluish-grey trilby hat to overcome the embarrassment. I constantly wore my new headgear wherever I went, as many people thought I might be a convict. From the 1980's a shorn head became quite fashionable and is a common sight to this present day.

As I gazed across the water, I was impressed at the sight of a huge ocean liner, decked with a large, squat, single funnel. It was our transport waiting to ship us home.

On the 7th August, we embarked with a number of other eager, excited passengers. A feeling of anticipation and soaring joy overcame me, as once again I trod on a ship's solid wooden decks. If all went well, my adventure could soon be at an end. I knew from my own experience however that, during times of war, nothing could be taken for granted.

The vessel was the former French owned "Pasteur" 29,253 grt, one of the largest liners in those days. I considered myself lucky to be one of the 1,829 passengers on board such a fine vessel. Her crew were mainly French, although she was managed by a British shipping company, the Cunard White Star, on behalf of the Ministry of War Transport.

I joined a long orderly queue, where a smart uniformed Purser and his assistant were allocating the accommodation. After checking the lists, a steward escorted us to our allotted small double cabin, situated well below decks. It was sparsely furnished, with two narrow beds, an upper and lower. I couldn't help remarking on the pure white linen, and the soft feather pillows. It was so tidy, spick and span, with nothing out of place. I thought we were in heaven. It was the absolute opposite of the sleeping arrangements we had endured recently, particularly in comparison to the unyielding bare boards of the Miranda prison camp.

The latest rumour being spread around was soon confirmed by the steward. The bad news was that no-one was allowed to go ashore. The good news was that departure was scheduled to take place very early the following morning. After settling in, we mixed amongst the joyful crowds in the beautifully furnished lounge. Groups of people had gathered there, noisily singing and dancing in celebration. Thirsty passengers constantly tried to place their orders with the harassed waiters. They struggled with fully loaded trays of drinks, attempting to make their way through the crowds of happy people. Later, the saloon was suddenly emptied as we answered the compulsory summons to lifeboat drill. As I collected and donned my life-jacket, it brought back vivid memories of the battle with the "Orion" in the Tasman Sea.

I abruptly noticed that I was silently counting the number of lifeboats stationed on the boat deck. I was calculating that half of them would be destroyed if we were attacked and was busy working out the consequences. Would there be enough to take off all the passengers and crew? I tried to banish these negative pictures from my mind, hoping and praying this emergency would not wreck the final part of my bid for freedom.

I stayed up on deck for a while, finding my way around the luxurious vessel, discovering the beautifully furnished amenities. I took a long walk around the crowded promenade deck and then joined a queue at the entrance to the dining room. Passengers were eagerly awaiting the sound of the dinner gong. After a sumptuous meal, served by friendly stewards attending to our every whim, I took another walk on the promenade deck. It was late evening, quiet and still, with few passengers about. I gazed all around at the eerie blackness of the Rock. In contrast, a short distance away, I could see the twinkling lights that illuminated the skies above the Spanish territory. Feeling very tired, I decided to turn in. Taking a last look around, I faced in the direction of Spain, and shouted loudly, "Adios Franco, Adios Espania!". Feeling much better having got that off my chest, I returned smiling to my cabin below.

Although sailing shortly, I felt calm and at ease as the earlier feelings of both excitement and expectation wore off. Preparing for bed, I changed into my striped cotton pyjamas. Then, neatly folding my new grey flannel trousers, I ensured the creases were in the right places. Looking at my two white shirts, socks, navy blue jacket, my new trousers and bright red tie, I had an enormous feeling of well-being. I was recovering my confidence and self respect. It was to be very many weeks though, before I finally discarded the trilby hat which hid my bald head. I expect that the final hair-shave, just before leaving, was the Spaniards' cruel sense of humour. Something to remember them by, at least for the next few months.

It was hard to believe we were on the final stage of our journey and we discussed our future plans. After a time, we became very tired and ready for sleep. I climbed the small ladder into my top bunk, pulling the crisp, laundered sheets and soft blankets around my shoulders. I said softly, "It won't be long now Frank, Bon Voyage". In a tired voice he whispered, "And the same to you Oz". I turned on my side, closed my eyes and soon fell into a deep untroubled sleep.

At 1am the following morning, the 8th August, I was awakened by a familiar sound. The noise and bustle of a ship leaving port. Under cover of darkness, the magnificent ship was slowly stealing away from her moorings. Obviously, the Germans were aware of the "Pasteur" being in Gibraltar, I was unsure what to expect. After leaving the comparative safety of the harbour, many debated whether on reaching the open seas, we might be attacked. It could come from enemy planes, surface warships or submarines. We could only wait and see.

I longed for the morning to arrive. At 7.30 am, I hurriedly showered and dressed and ran up on deck. The seas were very rough, but I didn't mind that. I thought

PASTEUR 1942

257

SIKH 1938

MAORI 1939

259

**LIGHTNING 1941**

261

we were probably still in the Straits of Gibraltar. As I scanned the seas, it was reassuring to see ahead, a huge British warship ploughing her way through the waves. It was the heavily armed battle cruiser HMS "Renown". Far in the distance were four other Royal Navy vessels. They were much smaller ships, all destroyer types, including HMS "Cossack", "Maori", "Sikh" and "Lightning". What a wonderful escort! I felt much more relaxed having the company and protection of five warships of the Royal Navy. Unfortunately, during the later war years, all four destroyers were lost through enemy action. The battleship "Renown" fared better, surviving the following four years of conflict.

On board the "Pasteur", the celebrations had worn off. Everyone was quieter and more subdued. We sailed steadily into the Atlantic Ocean and through the notoriously rough weather of the Bay of Biscay. There was a strong bracing wind and I enjoyed going for long walks on the promenade deck. Hours were spent swapping stories with other passengers. As each day passed, so the weather became cooler. Five uneventful days after leaving Gibraltar, we reached the north-west coast of Scotland.

THE NEW ZEALAND SHIPPING CO.LD.
(INCORPORATED IN NEW ZEALAND.)

TELEGRAPHIC ADDRESS,
"DELECTABLE, STOCK, LONDON."

TELEPHONE No.:5220 AVENUE.

ALL COMMUNICATIONS TO BE ADDRESSED
THE GENERAL MANAGERS

138, Leadenhall Street,
London, E.C.3.

13th August, 1941

Mrs. Sweeney,
    28, Nicholas Road,
        Dagenham.

Dear Mrs. Sweeney,

        We have been advised by the Admiralty that
"two survivors of the "TURAKINA" are expected to arrive
in Scotland today".  In view of the information which
we received from Gibraltar, we are assuming that these
will be your son and Mr. Quinn.

        We have made all arrangements for them to
be properly looked after and provided with cash, and
have asked that your son be sent through to London as soon
as possible.  He may be delayed for a day or two if
the Authorities in Glasgow want to hear his story there.

                    Yours faithfully,

263

# CHAPTER 13

## I BELONG TO GLASGOW

It was August 13th, in the late afternoon, when we at last moored in the Clyde. The following day I would be ashore in Gourock. It seemed strange that after more than 15 months of adventure and captivity, travelling all over the world, I'd returned to the very port where I first joined the ill-fated Turakina. It was peculiar, how events had turned full circle, as there were many other ports in Britain where we could have landed. Sailing through the English Channel and up the East coast would have been more hazardous though, with the Germans occupying France and Belgium.

All passengers would be staying on board till the morning, and there were loud celebrations going on in the lounge and bars. Not normally a drinking person, I decided to have an early night to prepare myself for the following day, guessing it would be a long tiring one. I did not sleep a great deal, due to the loud talking and singing of noisy people in the passageways outside. Lying awake in my bunk, pictures of the events of the past months flashed through my mind. I found it difficult to block these thoughts from my mind in order to sleep. The morning and daylight could not come quickly enough. Very soon my dreams of a joyous reunion would become a reality.

Next morning, seated in the packed dining room, I ordered a typical English breakfast, fried egg, bacon, toast and coffee. Quickly demolishing the meal, I hurried below to pack my few possessions. Although midsummer, it was a cold damp morning. Fortunately, I still possessed my trusty seaman's jersey. I never expected to wear it so soon after experiencing the stifling humid weather in Spain.

Early that Thursday morning a small steamer edged alongside and was quickly made fast. It was the cross channel boat, "Maid of Orleans", preparing to disembark the passengers from the "Pasteur". At last, it was time to go ashore. With approximately 2,500 people on board, including the passengers and crew, the decks soon became very crowded. Long queues formed as excited passengers jostled in their efforts to board the newly arrived tender. I stood at the rails with Frank, watching and waiting patiently until the congestion eased.

Aboard the "Maid of Orleans" we were met by immigration officials, but we still couldn't provide the means of identification they requested. I just had the certificate issued by the Spanish authorities at Miranda. However, we were expected, cleared by the NZSC and the Consulate in Madrid. A few notes were hurriedly jotted down, then after answering some simple questions, I walked quickly through the barrier. I was advised not to give too much information to inquisitive press reporters. It was important not to mention the conditions suffered in the Spanish camp. Lurid details might create added dangers for future prisoners.

At midday, we were at last ashore in Gourock. The next stage meant going through Customs. I gave him a wry smile when an Officer said, "Have you anything to declare?"

Various officials approached, including a representative from the New Zealand Shipping Company. We were provided with money and rail tickets to Glasgow, and soon alighted at the busy station. A young, fresh-faced reporter representing the Glasgow Herald made himself known. During the interview, I gave a brief outline of our adventures, but due to censorship, a condensed news item appeared in the daily newspaper.

While in Glasgow, we were congratulated and welcomed to the city by the Lord Provost, Sir Patrick Dollan. Our reporter friend had made arrangements for an overnight stay in the Blytheswood hotel in Sauchiehall Street. There was no charge, because the Herald would settle the account. We later decided to celebrate our homecoming with a few half pint glasses of light ale. The customers soon heard our story and provided an endless supply of beer and cigarettes. I did refuse the tots of whisky though, as the strong spirit was not to my liking. After a while we became rather merry, and loudly joined in the singing. There were repeated noisy choruses of "On the bonny banks of Loch Lomand", followed by hearty renderings of "I belong to Glasgow".

I succeeded in shaking off the amorous attentions of an attractive young Scotch lassie, intent on clasping her arms around my neck. She forcefully attempted to remove my hat, determined to expose the embarrassment of my shaven head. However, I was able to thwart her efforts. Later, when the bar closed, we retired to our cosy hotel room. That night I didn't need any rocking. Without a care in the world, I slept like the proverbial log.

Eventually, the time came for Frank and I to part company. At the station, we hugged warmly and shook hands. Frank later returned to his home and family in Lanark, Scotland, and I to Dagenham, in the County of Essex, England. We made plans to meet again as soon as possible. Unfortunately, after all the adventures and dangers we endured and overcome, we were destined never to meet or speak to each other again.

# "CIVVY STREET"

It was still daylight when I eventually reached my home. It was a rapturous feeling recognising friendly faces and seeing again the familiar surroundings. Nothing had changed. As I turned the corner of my road, an amazing sight greeted me. The usual drab appearance of identical houses on the estate, were transformed with a blaze of colour. My wonderful neighbours had hung flags and brightly coloured bunting along both sides of the street. A friend confided lights would have been erected, but they were prohibited. Because of the German air raids, there was a compulsory blackout after dark. Hanging across my house, a large sign flapping in the breeze, caught my eye. It said it all: "Welcome home Eddie".

A few days later I was summoned to Whitehall, London, to make a statement. I was debriefed at some length by a tall fair-haired man, wearing a smart civilian suit. His main concern was of the movements of the German raider "Orion". The War Office, like the Naval Attache in Spain, mainly required information of all the German ships involved. For the second time, I was advised to keep certain matters secret, particularly items relating to our internment in Spain.

Unlike Frank, I was not recalled for service, being directed by the Ministry of Labour to work in the London docks for Messrs Green and Siley Ware. Given a trial as a blacksmiths' hammerman, I was armed with a heavy, long handled hammer, which I had to swing and strike with a great deal of effort. The blacksmith, Arthur Heddle, using a long pair of tongs to hold the lumps of red-hot metal flat on his anvil. He would point to a particular spot and I would attempt to give it a whack with my hammer. Fortunately, most times I connected.

As the metal cooled, it was quickly reheated in the forge. On one occasion, I recall he was making a precision instrument, a pair of large callipers. The article was very skilfully completed. After a spell as a hammerman, I was promoted and spent some time working on a cutting machine, burning through metal to a specific pattern from a blueprint. After a few weeks working inside the shop, I was given a card by the manager Mr. Edwards, and informed I had been accepted as a member of a trade union, which I believe was the Forge and Smithy workers.

I was later put to work on ships in the docks. I felt at home and enjoyed working on board again. As well as a 4.7" gun mounted on the poop deck, all merchant ships were being armed with light anti-aircraft guns. My instructions were to help in heating, bending and welding together protective metal railings, measuring about one inch in diameter. In the excitement during an attack by enemy aircraft, the rails partly surrounding the gun, would prevent the ship's gunner accidentally firing on his own vessel or injuring members of his crew.

By the end of the war, British merchant ships sunk by enemy action amounted to 2562, with a total tonnage of 11,400,000 tons. Other Allied and neutral ships lost amounted to almost 10,000,000 tons. More than 35,000 British merchant seamen lost their lives through enemy action. Over 4,000 became prisoners and were held for the duration of the war. Some became very ill and did not survive. Other sick men were lucky enough to be repatriated in exchange for similar German prisoners from Britain. The remainder were released by the advancing Allied troops when the Germans were finally defeated.

On April 28th 1945, Italy's dictator leader, Benito Mussolini aged 62, was captured and executed by Italian Communist partisans. His body was hung in the street for all to see. In his early days he was a Marxist, but later gave up this ideology and entered the war on Hitler's side in 1940.

Adolph Hitler, aged 56, Germany's Nazi Chancellor, had evaded capture but on April 30th 1945, he committed suicide and his body found in a bunker in his Berlin headquarters. It occurred just as occupying Russian troops were storming the city. On May 23rd 1945, the day the Russians entered Berlin, the German High Co nmand were arrested and put in prison. While in jail, another prominent Nazi, Himmler, also committed suicide. The German casualties in the battle for that city amounted to 150,000 killed and 300,000 taken prisoner.

# THE CONCLUSION

In May 1995, with a friend Julie Marks, I drove from Calais to Ales in southern France, not far from Argeles. I was delighted to meet Jacqueline Soubrier, after a lapse of 54 years. Now a Grandmother, she is happily married to Jacques. Her first words were, "What kept you so long?" I didn't really know how to answer her, but it is something I regret did not happen earlier.

At the Chateaux Millemont, the original owners are deceased. However, the gatekeeper contacted the sole survivor and occupant, the only daughter of Ms. De Baudus. When I told her who I was she asked for the gates to be unlocked, allowing us to enter. We were escorted to the castle, invited into the lavishly furnished drawing room and made very welcome.

With the passing of time, it has been difficult tracing the French citizens who risked their lives in giving me valuable assistance. Without their aid, we may never have succeeded in evading capture. My heartfelt thanks goes to them all.

In 1940, my brother, A.B. William George Sweeney, aged 19 years, was killed on active duty overseas, when the destroyer HMS "Gallant", was bombed and sunk after an attack by the Italian Air Force.

This is the end of my story. Having led a full busy life, I've had little time to put pen to paper. Amazingly, the events that occurred so many years ago are still clear in my mind. Such traumatic moments will live forever. I have always considered myself very fortunate in not spending nearly five years as a prisoner of war in Germany.

The stories of bravery of Merchant seamen during the war have been well recorded. Although no match for the enemy surface warships, they provided a lifeline for the people of Great Britain. Submarines were another terrible hazard, sinking 2775 ships. However, the Merchant Navy, defying all odds, played a key role in helping to overcome the threat of Adolph Hitler and his Nazi forces.

I have retained my love of ships and the sea. In fact, for most of my life, I have lived within sight of the beach and harbour. Writing this book has resulted in the making of many new friends, home and abroad.

My only regret? I should have done it sooner.

E.J.S.

# FRANK QUINN

After a safe return to his home in Lanark, Frank was surprisingly called up for National Service. He was enlisted in the Ayrshire Yeomanry, attached to the Royal Artillery. Sent overseas, he served in France and Germany for another four years and fortunately survived the conflict without injury. At the cessation of hostilities in September 1945, he became a member of the Allied occupying forces, spending a considerable time in Germany. Later, on leaving the Army with an honourable discharge, he decided to opt for the Merchant Navy.

In October 1948, he rejoined the New Zealand Shipping Company. His new assignment, the M. V. "Haparangi" 11,281 tons, was similar to the "Turakina" in many ways. She was also a refrigerated vessel, carrying general cargo. A modern freighter at that time, she made regular runs between New Zealand and Britain, until sold and broken up in Taiwan in 1973. After about 6 more years service, Frank gave up the sea, settling down to a life ashore and for some years worked as a steel erector in Wales.

After a long illness, in 1964 his health deteriorated. Still a comparatively young man, he lost his fight to live. Married with one daughter, he had lived in Connahs Quay, near Flint in North Wales. I can only add that, during the good and bad times we shared together, there was never a cross word. Frank was a good friend, and will always be remembered.

# TURAKINA CREW KILLED IN ACTION

| | |
|---|---|
| J.B.Laird | Captain |
| H. Neagle | Chief Officer |
| J. Hudson | Second   Officer |
| K. Jones | First Radio Officer |
| J.W. Penny | Second Radio Officer |
| A. McK. Lloyd | Apprentice |
| E.N. Dean | Carpenter |
| W.J. Jolliffe | Boatswain |
| R. Norton | Able Seaman |
| J. Flaws | Able Seaman |
| L. Gorman | Able Seaman |

| | |
|---|---|
| E.T. Davis | Able Seaman |
| S. Foster | Ordinary Seaman |
| S.T. Manders | Ordinary Seaman |
| J. Abercrombie | Ordinary Seaman |
| M.A. Judge | Chief Cook |
| R. King | Second Cook |
| J.F. Smith | Butcher |
| C.T. Mays | Chief Engineer |
| C.W. Richings | Second Engineer |
| A. Overy | Third Engineer |
| G.H. Need | Fourth Engineer |
| C. McCree | Fifth Engineer |
| G.R. Francis | Sixth Engineer |

| | |
|---|---|
| S. Meldrum | Second Refrig. Engineer |
| E.H. Brotheridge | Donkeyman |
| J.T. Bright | Storeman |
| C.L. Colthurst | Greaser |
| C.W. Stokes | Greaser |
| E. Pinnington | Refrig. Greaser |
| R. Edwards | Refrig. Greaser |
| J. Maloney | Refrig. Greaser |
| T.P. Molloy | Fireman |
| M. Hazlett | Fireman |
| P. J. Brennan | Fireman |
| P.J. Carty | Asst. Steward |

**************************************

# TURAKINA CREW 1940

# PRISONERS OF WAR

| | |
|---|---|
| John Mallett | Third Officer |
| Henry Spencer | Fourth Officer |
| Alexander Grey | Chief Steward |
| Kenneth Upton | $2^{nd}$ Steward |
| L. Jervis | Mess Steward |
| Allan Slater | 7th Engineer |
| Claude Morris | 1st Refrig. Engineer |
| Alistair Taylor | App. Officer |
| James Burgess | A.B. Seaman |
| Charles Gillette | O. Seaman |

| | |
|---|---|
| Martin Hurley | O. Seaman |
| L.G. McGuail | Engine Room |
| Leslie Fisher | Engine Room |
| Micheal Dunn | Engine Room |
| William Curry | Engine Room |
| William Underwood | Mess Boy |
| Francis Quinn | O. Seaman<br>Escaped |
| E.J. Sweeney | Deck Boy<br>Escaped |
| Sydney Manders | O. Seaman.<br>Died on board<br>German Raider<br>Buried at sea |

\*\*\*\*\*\*\*\*\*\*\*\*\*\*\*\*\*\*\*\*\*\*\*\*\*\*\*\*\*\*\*\*\*\*\*\*\*\*\*\*

# THE TURAKINA

Turakina is the name of a small river in Taranaki, New Zealand and in the native Maori language means "fallen tree". Since 1868 five different vessels have at some time sailed under the name.


## TURAKINA No 1

Sailing vessel
| | |
|---|---|
| Builder | Charles Connell & Co. Glasgow Scotland |
| Order No. | 60352 |
| Yard No. | 55 |
| Completed | May 1868 |
| Weight | GRT 1247 tons. Nett 1189 tons. |
| Length | 232.5. Beam 35.4. Depth 22.2 |
| Registration | London England |
| Completed as | City of Perth for Robert Smith & Sons Glasgow. |
| Sold 1870 to | Geo. Smith & Sons Glasgow. Name unchanged. |
| Sold 1879 to | James Clark Glasgow. Name unchanged. |
| Sold 1881 to | William Service Glasgow. Name unchanged. |
| Sold 1882 to | New Zealand Shipping Co Ltd Lyttelton Name later changed to Turakina. |
| Registration | 1887 London England. |
| Sold 1899 to | Acties Elida, Renamed Elida. Registration Tvedestrand Norway. Managers Alexander Bech |
| Sold May 1914 | Broken up. |

## TURAKINA No. 2

| | |
|---|---|
| Builder | Hawthorn Leslie & Co. Ltd. Newcastle. |
| Order No. | 114620 |
| Yard No. | 382 |
| Completed | August 1902 |
| Engine | T6 cy. 922 NHP. |
| Screws | Twin |
| Engine Builder | Hawthorn Leslie Co. Ltd. |
| Weight | Gross tonnage 9920, Nett 6351. |
| Length | 473.00,   Beam 59.60, Depth 31.00 |
| First World War | 1914 - 1918. August 13th 1918. Attacked by German submarine. Torpedoed and sunk 120 miles W.S.W. from Bishops Rock and the Isle of Scilly. Two crew members killed during the action. |

## TURAKINA No. 3

| | |
|---|---|
| Builder | William Hamilton & Co. Ltd. Glasgow. |
| O/N | 145988 |
| Yard No. | 322 |
| Completed | September 1923 |
| Engines | 2 Steam turbines. S. R. Geared |
| Screws | Single |
| Speed | 15 Knots |
| Engine Builder | D. Rowan & Co. Ltd. Glasgow. |
| Weight | Gross 9691.  Nett 6093.  DWT 11780 |
| Length | 460.50. Beam 62.70. Depth 35.20 |
| Registration | Plymouth. England. Second World War 1939 - 1945. |
| 20-8-1940 | Attacked by German Raider in Tasman Sea. Position.   38-33-00-S-167-12-00-E. |
| 20-8-1940. | Sunk. Position 38-27-00-S-167-35-00-E. |

## TURAKINA No. 4

| | |
|---|---|
| Builder | Bartram & Sons Ltd. Sunderland. |
| O/N | 301224 |
| Completed | September 1960. |
| Yard No. | 384 |
| Engine Builder | George Clark (Sunderland) Ltd. |
| BHP | 10400 |
| GRT | 7707  Nett. 3973  DWT 8600 |
| Length | 454.11  Width 66.2  Depth 38.0 |
| Built for | New Zealand Shipping Co. Ltd. |
| Registration | London. England. 1967 to Federal Steam Navigation Ltd. |
| Managers | New Zealand Shipping Co. |
| Registration | London. England. |
| October 1971 | New Managers. P&O General Cargo Division. |
| April 1973 | New Owners. P&O Steam Navigation Co. |
| P.O.Reg. London. | P&O General Cargo Division. |
| Sold | August 1977 Uiterwyk Line (Reefer) inc. |
| Registration | Monrovia Liberia. Name unchanged. Later 1978 Renamed Patricia U. |
| Sold | 1978 Sparta Shipping Co. S.A. Same name. Place of registration not known. |
| Sold | 1982 Armadora Compania Frigorifica. S.A. P.O.R. not known. Renamed Gulf Reefer. |
| Sold | 1985 to unknown Maltese owners. P.O.R not known. Name changed to Ren-Sines. |
| Sold | 1986 to Chinese shipbreakers arriving Huangpu, China on 17th January 1986. |

From 20-6-83 to 13-11-85 she had been laid up at Astakos Greece.

281

## M.V. TURAKINA  No. 5

Builders          J.J.Sietas KG Shiffswerft. GmbH & Co.
                  Hamburg Germany.
Yard No.          939
Delivery date     10th October 1983
Owner             Reederel Bernd KG. MS "Amd Becker",
                  Jork.
Agents            South Pacific Shipping Ltd.
                  Christchurch.
Port of Reg.      Hamburg Germany.
Class             Container-Transport + MC AUT
Tonnage           1599.90. GRT. 1118.48 NRT.  DWT
                  4644T
Speed             15 Knots
Engine            1 KND diesel type SBV 8M 540
                  2900 KW at 600/148 min-1
                  1 reduction gear
Screws            1 controllable pitch propeller
Equipment         Bow thruster 220 KW, 2 radars, gyro
                  compass, auto pilot, direction finder
                  and echo sounder.
Hatches           2 only, 25.16 x 12.5m each
                  Cargo Capacity   Grain 6569.5 m3
                  Bale 6286.4 m3

1998              Turakina still in service.

# SHIPS OF THE NEW ZEALAND SHIPPING CO.

| | | |
|---|---|---|
| Tongariro | 4,163 tons | 1883-1899 |
| Aorangi | 4,163 | 1883-1889 |
| Ruapehu | 4,163 | 1883-1889 |
| Rimutaka | 4,474 | 1885-1900 |
| Kaikoura | 4,474 | 1894-1907 |
| Papanui | 6,372 | 1898-1911 |
| Whakatane | 5,629 | 1900-1924 |
| Rimutaka | 7,665 | 1900-1930 |
| Ruapehu | 7,885 | 1901-1931 |
| Tongariro | 8,073 | 1901-1916 |
| Turakina | 9,691 | 1902-1917 |
| Kaipara | 7,392 | 1903-1914 |
| Opowa | 7,230 | 1906-1928 |
| Otaki | 7,420 | 1907-1917 |
| Ruahine | 10,832 | 1909-1949 |
| Remuera | 11,445 | 1911-1940 |
| Rotorua | 11,911 | 1911-1940 |
| Hororata | 9,178 | 1913-1943 |
| Otaki | 7,976 | 1920-1934 |
| Otarama | 7,753 | 1920-1928 |
| Tekoa | 8,531 | 1922-1958 |
| Turakina | 8,565 | 1923-1940 |
| Tongariro | 8,719 | 1924-1960 |
| Rangitata | 16,737 | 1929-1962 |
| Rangitane | 16,712 | 1929-1940 |
| Rangitiki | 16,698 | 1929-1962 |
| Otaio | 10,048 | 1930-1941 |
| Opawa | 10,017 | 1931-1942 |
| Rimutaka | 16,385 | 1923-1950 |
| Kajoara | 5,882 | 1938-1955 |

| | | |
|---|---|---|
| Kaipaki | 5,862 | 1939-1955 |
| Hororata | 12,090 | 1942-1967 |
| Paparoa | 10,006 | 1944-1970 |
| Pipiriki | 10,065 | 1944-1971 |
| Rakaia | 8,213 | 1946-1971 |
| Haparangi | 11,281 | 1947-1973 |
| Hinakura | 11,272 | 1949-1974 |
| Hurunui | 11,276 | 1949-1973 |
| Rangitoto | 21,809 | 1949-1969 |
| Rangitane | 21,809 | 1950-1968 |
| Remuera | 13,362 | 1948-1969 |
| Turakina | 7,707 | 1960-1977 |
| Piako | 9,986 | 1962-1979 |
| Taupo | 8,200 | 1966-1980 |
| Tekoa | 8,200 | 1966-1980 |
| Tongariro | 8,200 | 1966-1980 |
| Mataura | 8,000 | 1968-1977 |
| Manapouri | 8,000 | 1968-1977 |

\*\*\*\*\*\*\*\*\*\*\*\*\*\*\*\*\*\*\*\*\*\*\*\*\*\*\*\*\*\*\*\*\*\*\*\*\*\*\*\*\*\*\*\*\*\*\*\*\*\*\*\*\*\*\*\*\*\*\*\*\*\*

1930 CLASS PHOTOGRAPH TAKEN AT NOTT STREET STATE SCHOOL, PORT MELBOURNE
E. J. SWEENEY WEARING WHITE SHIRT

EDWARD J. SWEENEY, TAKEN 1937 IN HIS HOME TOWN OF PORT MELBOURNE

A RECENT PICTURE TAKEN OF THE AUTHOR, EDWARD J. SWEENEY